DIRECT MAIL
in the
DIGITAL AGE

Lin Grensing-Pophal, PCM

DIRECT MAIL *in the* DIGITAL AGE

Self-Counsel Press
(a division of)
International Self-Counsel Press Ltd.
USA   Canada

Self-Counsel Press acknowledges the financial support of the Government of Canada through the Canada Book Fund (CBF) for our publishing activities.

Printed in Canada.

First edition: 2011

Library and Archives Canada Cataloguing in Publication

Grensing-Pophal, Lin, 1959–

   Direct mail in the digital age / Lin Grensing-Pophal.

   ISBN 978-1-77040-071-9

   1. Advertising, Direct-mail. 2. Small business — Management.
I. Title.

| HF5861.G726 2011 | 659.13'3 | C2010-906864-5 |

Cover Image
Copyright©iStockphoto/Check Your Mail/Bluberries

Every effort has been made to obtain permission for quoted material. If there is an omission or error, the author and publisher would be grateful to be so informed.

Self-Counsel Press
(a division of)
International Self-Counsel Press Ltd.

1704 North State Street	1481 Charlotte Road
Bellingham, WA 98225	North Vancouver, BC V7J 1H1
USA	Canada

Contents

Notice to Readers

Laws are constantly changing. Every effort is made to keep this publication as current as possible. However, the author, the publisher, and the vendor of this book make no representations or warranties regarding the outcome or the use to which the information in this book is put and are not assuming any liability for any claims, losses, or damages arising out of the use of this book. The reader should not rely on the author or the publisher of this book for any professional advice. Please be sure that you have the most recent edition.

Introduction

Back in 1923, Claude C. Hopkins, widely recognized as a great advertising pioneer, wrote in *Scientific Advertising*: "The severest test of an advertising man is in selling goods by mail. But that is a school from which he must graduate before he can hope for success. There cost and results are immediately apparent. False theories melt away like snowflakes in the sun. The advertising is profitable or it is not, clearly on the face of returns."

In 1991, I wrote: "Direct mail was the shining star of advertising in the 1980s and promises to continue to be so in the 1990s. It's the fastest growing form of advertising because it's measurable, relatively easy to produce, and cost effective." Fast forward about 20 years and I could probably say exactly the same thing about e-marketing. How the world has changed!

While the delivery mechanisms are different, in reality, the basics of communicating effectively with whoever the target audience might be really haven't changed very much, if at all. Effective communication is still effective communication, and direct mail — whether in the snail mail environment or online — still benefits from the same tried and true principles that gurus such as Claude C. Hopkins, and later, Bob Bly and Herschell Gordon Lewis espoused and practiced.

When you run a radio spot for your product or service it's hard to tell exactly how effective it is. When you mail coupons to prospects — whether delivered via snail mail or email — it's easy to measure the results; simply count the coupons you get back. Better yet, in the digital age, you can tell how many people opened your email, how many forwarded it on to others, how many clicked through to various parts of the message, and (based on their email addresses or domains) who they are!

Truly, the beauty of direct mail is its measurability — the ability for marketers to know, with certainty, the value of the effort they have put forth. That same thing can't be said about other forms of advertising. While success may be implied, it cannot be explicitly measured when we use techniques such as television advertising, billboards, print advertising, etc.

Regardless of what you have to sell or who you want to sell it to, direct mail (traditional and/or digital-era) can provide a flexible, measurable, and very cost-effective means of delivering your message and achieving results.

Those who are already steeped in the practice of traditional direct mail will find that there aren't a lot of differences between the traditional and the new-media approach. Those who have not yet dipped their toes into direct mail marketing will be glad to learn that the principles can be readily applied whether they're developing materials for delivery to a mailbox or a desktop.

It sounds simple enough and it really is. The information in this book will make it easy for you to plan and produce your own direct-mail campaigns, measure their results, and make improvements to subsequent campaigns to generate even better results. That's the beauty of direct mail!

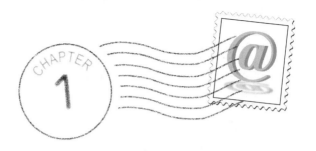

Beginnings and Benefits

irect mail can be simply defined as mail that is delivered directly to a single, intended recipient. It is direct and it uses the mail. Traditionally, in business-to-consumer environments, this has meant mail delivered to a mailbox. In business-to-business environments, mail is delivered to business addresses, post office boxes, etc., and is often sorted, managed, and distributed by mail rooms. Today it means mail delivered electronically to email inboxes or social media accounts.

Direct mail is a form of direct marketing. Lester Wunderman is widely considered to be the creator of modern-day direct marketing. Wunderman was born in 1920, is still alive as of this writing, and introduced marketers to such innovations as the magazine subscription card, the toll-free number, and loyalty rewards programs. He coined the term "direct marketing" in 1967.

Direct marketing is marketing that is directed at a specific group of individuals and intended to elicit an immediate response (e.g., placement of an order or generation of an inquiry). In fact, the basic requirement for a marketing effort to be classified as *direct* marketing is that the response be direct and immediate. General advertising, by way of comparison, is designed to convince consumers to make a purchase *at some later date*. On the one hand, when you watch a commercial for Target, the people who developed the commercial don't expect you to immediately jump up, get in your car, and drive to Target. Direct marketing, on the other hand, is designed to elicit just such an immediate response.

1. Direct Marketing Techniques

Direct marketing may use one or more of the following techniques:

- Telephone
- Television
- Print advertisements
- Direct mail
- Digital direct mail
- Billboards

All of these are examples of direct marketing efforts that are designed to achieve an immediate (or almost immediate) response from a group of consumers. The following sections discuss these direct marketing techniques.

1.1 Telephone

You're sitting down to eat dinner when the phone rings. You answer it and, to your chagrin, it's a telemarketer trying to sell you something. This time that "something" is a magazine that you are really interested in and the price is right. You bite. Some clever businessperson just used telephone direct marketing to reach right into your home and make a sale.

While telephone solicitation, or telemarketing, is not direct mail, it does share one important element with direct mail — the need for a list of individuals who are likely to be interested in what the marketer has to sell. This is not true of other forms of direct marketing, as we'll see.

Telephone direct marketing has the advantages of immediacy and personal interaction with the potential customer, but many people feel telephone marketing is intrusive and they will react negatively to a phone call. In addition, some offers are too complex to be explained adequately in a short phone conversation. Add to that the movement away from traditional land lines to mobile telephones.

1.2 Television

It's late and you can't sleep. The program you're watching is interrupted by a musical performer from days gone by strumming a guitar and promoting a collection of greatest hits. To order, all you have to do is call a toll-free number now.

Or, you're watching what you think is a regular program, only to discover that you're in the midst of a long commercial known as an infomercial. The infomercial idea is not new; only the name is. The 30-minute commercial actually emerged in the 1950s. As programming time became harder and harder to get, the Federal Trade Commission outlawed these commercials. Now, however, with the renaissance of cable networks, they have become a staple of the airwaves.

Television direct marketing offers the strong impact of both visual and auditory messages at the same time. It is, however, much more expensive than other forms of direct marketing, and although some cable stations now offer marketers the opportunity to target specific market segments, the message will still reach a large number of people who are not part of your desired target audience.

1.3 Print advertisements

You're flipping through a magazine when your attention is caught by an interesting ad for product XYZ. To order, all you have to do is call a convenient 800-number or visit a website.

Print ads can be an inexpensive way of doing direct marketing, and the wide variety of consumer, trade, and technical publications offer marketers the opportunity to target specific market segments. However, a print ad in a multipage publication is competing with many other messages (including other ads) for the reader's attention. Also, news about the decline in subscriptions means fewer potential readers for your marketing messages.

1.4 Direct mail

Direct mail, a subset of direct marketing, takes this concept one step further by targeting specific individuals with an appeal to "act now." The big benefit of direct mail has always been the ability to target a specific message to a specific individual. Unlike mass-media marketing (i.e., television advertising), which is distributed to the masses, direct mail has the advantage of allowing the marketer to define a market based on various demographic and psychographic attributes and target specific messages to that market on a one-to-one basis.

With direct mail, your marketing dollars aren't wasted as they might be in other forms of advertising because you're targeting your promotion specifically to those people who will be most interested in your product. Let's take a look at a simple comparison:

You're selling a line of clothing for pregnant women. You could advertise on television — perhaps a spot on a cable network during a program whose audience is primarily women in their childbearing years. The key word here is *primarily*. Why? Because, in addition to these viewers, there will undoubtedly be female viewers outside this age group, as well as men and children. Even the women who are in their childbearing years may very well not be pregnant (or not planning to become pregnant) at the time your commercial is airing. But, you're paying to reach all of these viewers. You are, in effect, throwing a portion of your money away.

If you were using direct mail, however, you could find and purchase a list of women who subscribe to a magazine specifically for pregnant women. Or, a list of women who have purchased maternity clothes from another manufacturer. You pay only to reach those people you identify as prime targets for your advertising message.

Better yet, today the concept of direct mail has evolved to incorporate online mail (i.e., email) delivered to the inboxes of both consumer and business audiences.

1.5 Digital direct mail

Digital marketing (like direct marketing) is a broader term that encompasses online direct mail (or email) marketing, as well as the use of websites, blogs, social media, etc., to market products and services. Digital direct mail, like traditional direct mail, is a subset that is differentiated on the basis of specifically targeting individuals through the delivery of messages via email or online communication through various social media channels (e.g., Twitter, Facebook, LinkedIn) which targets them individually.

1.6 Billboards

Billboards or other forms of outdoor advertising can be used to elicit a direct response from consumers who drive or ride by the signage on a regular basis. Advertisers will evaluate traffic patterns to carefully consider the placement of these messages, which are often coordinated as part of a larger campaign that might also have messages in other media. An example of how this was done quite effectively is 1-800-FLOWERS; their phone number is an integral part of their messaging and is used to encourage direct response.

2. Digital versus Traditional Direct Mail

There is much more that is the same than is different between traditional direct mail marketing and digital email marketing. In fact, the primary difference is the distribution method — mail delivered to a traditional mailbox versus mail delivered online in electronic format. The basics still apply. You need to do the following:

1. Identify your overall goals and objectives.

2. Identify your target audience.

3. Identify your strategies and tactics (i.e., traditional or electronic direct mail or a combination of both) that will be most effective for you based on your goals, objectives, and target audience.

4. Create the offer.

5. Select, locate, and rent or purchase lists.*

6. Develop key messages or copy points.

7. Choose format options.*

8. Design materials.*

9. Distribute your promotion — either through the postal system or online.*

10. Evaluate the results.

As we explore each of these traditional steps in the chapters ahead, we'll identify any issues that may be different between traditional and electronic direct mail marketing.

3. The State of the Direct Mail Industry

In 1897, Mark Twain was quoted by the *New York Journal*, in response to rumors of his death, as saying: "The report of my death was an exaggeration." Interesting how rumors could spread even before the days of mass communication and electronic communication. This quote has additional relevance for us because it could similarly be said of traditional direct mail marketing.

---

* **Note:** The points above that will have the most variation are 5, 7, 8, and 9. The others are the same. So, if you've been successful at traditional direct mail marketing, you're already well on your way toward achieving success online!

Many have lamented direct mail's passing and, in truth, the US Postal Service has struggled in recent years to recapture revenue lost by the decline in traditional mailed correspondence to more online communication. Despite the US Postal Service delivering approximately 170 billion pieces of mail in 2010, it lost about $6 billion in revenue, making mail volume about 7 billion pieces fewer than in 2009, according to a release by Postmaster General John E. Potter in October, 2010. Much of that decline can be attributable to the shift from traditional direct mail to online options that can take advantage of significant savings, not only in postage but in print production costs as well.

Still, despite the dire prognostications, the Direct Marketing Association's "2010 Response Rate Trend Report" pointed out that response rates for direct mail have stayed steady over the past four years. For example, letter-sized envelopes had a response rate in 2010 of 3.42 percent for a house list and 1.38 percent for a prospect list. (See Chapter 4 for more information about lists.) Catalogs had the lowest cost per lead of $47.61, ahead of inserts at $47.69, email at $53.85, and postcards at $75.32.

Consider also, the ability to use direct mail to provide product samples (a proven and very effective marketing technique with a long history), and to deliver three-dimensional packages that attract attention and virtually demand to be opened.

According to a research study produced in cooperation with the Direct Marketing Association and sponsored by DiscMail Direct, DVDs and compact discs (CDs) are an example of a direct mail effort that yields significantly higher results than print media or email. The study, released in 2010, found the following:

- 91 percent of all respondents who received a DVD or CD in the mail opened the mailer

- 73 percent played the discs in their computers

- 59 percent thought a DVD was more secure than an email

- Respondents were 85 percent more likely to prefer receiving a DVD or CD in the mail than an email by the same advertiser

- 89 percent said they would spend more time, or the same amount of time, with a direct mail piece if it included a DVD or CD

Despite the fact that marketers could deliver the *exact same experience* online through a click of the mouse, there's just something about a tangible package that has yet to be replaced in the digital environment.

Traditional direct mail is inexpensive and effective. Aside from online marketing, it is still the most trackable means of communicating with a prospect, and it is still the most effective way to get an unsolicited message into consumers' hands where they're going to see it, even if they throw it away.

As with Twain, the report of the death of direct mail may certainly be an exaggeration. In fact, as more and more marketers bring their messages online and clutter up the mailboxes of their intended recipients, some will begin to take advantage of the relative "emptiness" of the old snail mail box. Here are some representative comments from participants in an online marketing forum:

- "My clients use direct mail every month to gain new customers and interact with existing customers. They mail from 50,000 to 500,000 pieces per month. They make money. Their customers love getting direct mail. It's personal, interactive, engaging, and extremely satisfying."

- "I prefer snail mail because my spam filter generally filters out more than 90 percent of the direct mail that comes electronically and I nuke the balance if I don't already know the person sending it. At least snail mail gets to the mailbox of the targeted consumer and needs a look to decide to recycle it."

- "Nothing captures my attention better than a well-written and engaging direct mail letter. Personal, well-crafted communication which stands out from the crowd is infinitely more compelling than a faceless, carbon-copied, email."

- "Direct mail isn't taking its last breath any time soon, but it is evolving. Business marketing strategies are different than they were even four or five years ago. Now it's common and necessary to integrate a marketing campaign with your website, social media pages, and email marketing. For example, you send a direct mail postcard to your target market, they go to a landing page where you offer a report or special discount and they, in turn, enter their contact info. Next you follow up with those contacts via email to stay in front of the new lead. It's a cycle that works together, and comes full circle, to close a sale. Bottom line: Direct mail still yields results, is effective for a variety of industries today, and is still one of the only mediums that can specifically target your ideal clients."

Karen Menachof, Chief Client Officer of Catalyst, a direct marketing firm in Rochester, New York, says, "Direct mail has always been the one channel where truly relevant information could be used by marketers to engage customers and prospects in a compelling manner to provide things that matter to them and thereby create true value while reinforcing the marketer's brand. Data-driven insights have long been the key driver to success in this channel."

What's really changed now that the digital marketplace seems to have taken over? Menachof says, "Sure, some folks no longer check their mail — some even opt out of receiving it entirely. Sure, many folks are more likely to actively seek information online rather than wait for it to arrive in their mailbox. Sure, some folks view direct mail as an obsolete channel. But the truth is that the direct mail channel is keeping up with the times. Our ability to further customize direct mail communications based on what we now know about their cross-channel interactions with us has the potential to make it more relevant than ever. And as we get better at understanding the preferences of those we are marketing to and are able to identify those individuals who prefer mail and/or those circumstances which justify mail we may mail less, but with exceptionally more impact. Mail is not dead, but its success is increasingly dependent on the effective integration of all channels so that the individual's needs are understood and addressed in the most relevant, impactful manner possible."

Menachof's final sentence is the key. While this book will deal specifically with direct mail which, as we've already seen, is a subset of direct marketing (which is a subset of promotion, one of the four Ps of the marketing mix that also includes product, price, and place), no individual promotional tool can or should be considered in a vacuum. To be most effective, marketers must consider the broad range of communication options available to them and then select the right *mix* of options to best meet their goals. In this book, we will focus specifically on the mix between traditional and digital email options. Still, many of the questions asked will be pertinent to marketing communication considerations in general.

What your prospects and customers will see of your direct mail is the actual presentation of your message, whether in letter, brochure, catalog, three-dimensional, DVD or CD, or electronic format. Before you even begin considering the development of what will become the final deliverable to your target audience, there are a lot of behind the scenes decisions and work that need to occur. The first consideration, identifying overall goals and objectives, is discussed in Chapter 2.

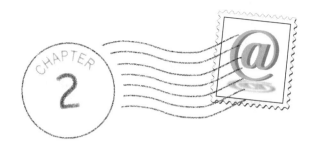

Identifying Your Overall
Goals and Objectives

B efore you can even begin to think about the specifics of your direct mail campaign, you need to determine what your goals and objectives are. You may want to —

- develop new markets,

- increase awareness of your company name,

- secure leads for your sales force, or

- increase sales.

The choice is yours — the key is to be specific.

Perhaps you're currently selling lawn and garden equipment and would like to add a line of sporting goods, or you're running webinars for administrative assistants and would like to introduce a new line of programming for a management-level audience. In each of these cases, your advertising objective might be to develop new markets through the acquisition of a certain number of prospects and/or customers.

If you use a direct sales force for some of your marketing efforts, you may want to qualify prospects rather than having your salespeople make cold calls. Direct mail can help you identify people who have an interest in your product or service before you send a salesperson to the phones or out on the road.

However, the most common objective for direct mailers is simply to generate sales. They want more people to spend more money on their products and services. While your objectives may change from one campaign to the next, it's important that you do take the time to identify a *quantifiable* objective for each of your direct mail efforts. Since the big benefit of direct mail is its measurability, you want to take full advantage of the ability to leverage this benefit through a solid foundation based on specific, quantifiable, and measurable goals. After all, if you don't know where you're going, any road will take you there.

1. Will Direct Mail Work for You?

Not everything will prove to be a successful mail-order product. Will your product sell through the mail? The following sections include five important questions to ask before embarking on a direct mail campaign. If you can answer "yes" to each of these questions, there's a good chance that your campaign can be a successful one.

1.1 Can you reach your market effectively through direct mail?

You will need to consider whether you can reach your market effectively through direct mail. Suppose you're selling a product that appeals to lawyers. It's easy enough to get a list of lawyers. You can reach your market. However, suppose you're selling a product that appeals to 30-year-old redheads who collect stamps. You're going to have a very tough time finding a list of these prospects (although tools such as Facebook Ads make this more of a possibility than in the past). Even if you were able to find a list of this target group, the number of potential customers will be so small that you may not be able to sell very large quantities of your product.

As we'll see, in direct mail the list is the most important aspect of your marketing effort. If you can't reach your market (e.g., if you can't find a list or enough lists), you can't sell your product.

Despite the cautions in the following sections, and even though you may not be able to *sell* every product or service through a direct mail effort, what you can often do is *generate qualified leads*. Having qualified leads can then become part of your sales pipeline, providing salespeople with names of individuals or companies that have expressed some interest or affinity that suggests they might be a good candidate for a follow-up call or visit.

1.2 Does your product have broad appeal?

Clothing has broad appeal. Everybody wears clothes. Many people buy clothes for fun, or to be fashionable, and these people buy clothes again and again because their old wardrobes become dated, or because they want to have more fun or be more fashionable! Even those who wear clothing strictly for utilitarian purposes need new clothes when theirs wear out. Clothing is also a common gift item.

Again, it gets down to the potential size of your market. The bigger the potential market, the greater the potential for higher volumes of sales. Direct mail is, more than anything, a numbers game.

1.3 Does your product stand out from the crowd?

Direct mail is easy to do, particularly in the digital age. That means that if you have competitors — and just about everybody has competitors — and direct mail is a viable marketing communication option for your product or service, your competitors are likely to be using direct mail as well. So you will need to stand out in some manner from your competition in terms of product quality, price point, access, or service (or some combination of these).

1.4 Can you describe or illustrate your product effectively through direct mail?

Clothing can be sold readily via direct mail because it's relatively easy to describe or illustrate through photographs. However, selling houses through the mail is more challenging. Why? Because houses are more complex and require more personal involvement on the part of the buyer to make a decision. In fact, the need for involvement tends to increase along with the dollar value of the item being considered for purchase. The higher the cost, the more the consumer will want to have an opportunity to see, examine, experience, and ask questions about the product. That's more than you can hope to do through a single direct mail effort.

1.5 Can you make a profit?

In the past, if your product sold for less than $15 and you only had one product to sell, you probably wouldn't be able to justify the cost of a direct mail campaign, which would include the cost of developing, printing, and mailing your direct mail piece as well as the cost of renting a list. Those days are gone, though, thanks to the advent of digital direct mail. In fact, one of the big benefits of email marketing is the low cost, since the cost of print and postage have literally been eliminated.

2. Goals

Determining whether your direct mail effort will be designed to generate sales, leads, or something else is part of the goal-setting process.

Goals are high-level statements of some end result you hope to achieve. Your direct mail goals might be to —

- generate qualified leads,
- increase sales, or
- increase your prospect/mailing list.

Your goal statement simply indicates what it is you hope to achieve with your direct mail effort. You can be more specific in your goal statement by including an indication of the target audience you're selecting. For example, your statements might include:

- Generate qualified leads in a certain geographic area or among a certain demographic segment.
- Increase sales to new customers, to customers who haven't purchased over a certain period of time, or to a new category of customers.
- Increase the number of CEOs or purchasing managers who sign up for your mailing list.

Table 1 includes some actual goal statements from direct mail campaigns.

TABLE 1
Goal Statements from Direct Mail Campaigns

Type of Business or Service	Goal
Dental clinic	Increase new patients.
Insurance company	Increase revenue and new clients.
Physical therapy services	Raise awareness of practice and increase new patients.
Jewelry	Increase attendance and sales at jewelry shows.

Party rental	Gain recognition for the business and attract more walk-in clients and web visitors.
Men's clothing	Increase sales.

Hopefully, what you'll notice from all of these examples is that while they are specific and provide an indication of what the marketer hopes to achieve through the direct mail effort, they are not measurable. By *how much* does the marketer wish to increase new patients, and what type of new patients does he or she want? By what date? That's okay. These are goals. Specificity is good, but one thing that goals do *not* do is indicate a specific numeric target or quantifiable end point. That's what objectives are for.

3. Objectives

Objectives are the quantifiable element of your direct mail campaign. What, specifically, is it that you hope to achieve? The great benefit of direct mail being measurable has already been mentioned, but you don't just measure your efforts *after* the campaign is over. You need to think about what it is you want to measure *before* the campaign begins. In short, what will success look like for you? How will you know if your campaign has been an effective one? The only way you can answer these questions is to establish specific objectives.

The key difference between goals and objectives is that goals provide a general direction but not enough specificity so that after the campaign is over, two independent people could say "Yes, we did it," or "No, we didn't."

Consider the dental clinic's goal in Table 1 of increasing new patients. Suppose the first day after the direct mail campaign goes out a new patient calls for an appointment. Does that mean the effort was a success? The goal has been met, after all. But no, of course it doesn't. Objectives are designed to create specificity around goals. Good objectives are stated in such a way that after the campaign is over, two or more individuals looking at the results can say "Yes, we were a success" or "No, we didn't achieve our objectives." A great acronym that can help marketers develop effective objectives is SMART, which stands for Specific, Measurable, Attainable, Realistic, and Time bound.

3.1 Objectives must be specific

We've already seen that "increase sales" is not specific enough to qualify as a good objective. A specific objective includes distinct details. Here's an example we can all relate to: losing weight. "Lose weight" is not specific, but "lose 15 pounds" is. Here are some other examples:

- Increase sales by 15 percent.
- Generate 500 leads.
- Add 2,000 names to the e-letter mailing list.

Which ones do you feel are good objectives? Actually, this is a trick question. While each of the above statements are specific, they are not yet effective objectives. Each of the statements could still be *more* specific. Again, think in terms of what might happen after the campaign as you and another member of your team — or your boss — sit down to discuss results. Let's reconsider these statements:

- Increase sales by 15 percent. Sales of what? All products? Specific products?
- Generate 500 leads. Any leads? Leads from a certain geographic area? Among a certain target demographic group?
- Add 2,000 names. What kind of names? Any names? Your Facebook friends' names or names of specific individuals with a specific level of buying power or potential?

Being as specific as possible gives you a good direction for developing your direct mail effort — it helps you to focus. It also helps to avoid misunderstanding and potential conflict later should you find that your expectations are different than others' expectations about the campaign.

Being specific is just the first step in developing effective objectives. There are other criteria that you need to consider, so read on to find out more.

3.2 Objectives must be measurable

There needs to be a way for you to determine at the end of the campaign whether or not you achieved success. For instance, "Increase repeat purchases from existing customers by 15 percent," is an objective that can be measured. "Create a high-impact direct mail campaign" is an example of an objective that is not currently stated in a measurable way. What is "high impact"? Who will judge whether or not the campaign is high impact? How will you quantify the evaluation?

The key here is to ask yourself: "Based on this statement, how will I measure whether or not the objective has been achieved?" If you can't come up with an answer, you don't have a measurable objective.

In addition to the question of whether or not it can be measured, marketers need to consider the ease or cost of measuring the desired results. In direct mail this is generally very straightforward — you can measure the number of responses, number of sales, etc. An objective related to raising awareness, though, might be more difficult and costly to measure. You would need to establish some form of baseline level of awareness among your target audience (perhaps through a survey), conduct the direct mail effort, and then remeasure awareness to see if there has been a change in the level of awareness.

Having to establish new processes or dedicate additional staff to measure whether or not you're achieving your objectives needs to be carefully considered to determine whether the knowledge gained will be worth the investment of time. Again, direct mail marketing efforts, unlike other forms of marketing, tend to readily lend themselves to cost-effective measurement.

3.3 Objectives must be attainable

Your objectives should represent attainable outcomes — results that you can reasonably expect to achieve. Consider how this might work on a personal level. A 120-pound woman would not set an objective of losing 50 pounds. That is not an attainable or realistic objective. She might, however, set a goal of losing 10 pounds.

The decision of whether or not an objective represents an attainable outcome can be a judgment call. In fact, often the "A" in the SMART acronym is said to stand for "agreed-upon," which is another important consideration. Your company leaders, project team, and any others with a stake in the outcome of your efforts need to agree upon the objectives you establish. That agreement will generally revolve around whether the objective is deemed to be attainable. In reaching agreement on objectives it is important to also consider the resources required to achieve the objective. A significant increase in sales, for example, might require the production of more products, put extra demand on shipping and customer service staff, and perhaps cause an increase in product returns.

3.4 Objectives must be realistic/relevant

Objectives are designed to support the goals that have been established. Therefore, objectives need to be aligned with or directly connected to those goals. Let's look at a couple of examples:

- Goal: To expand market share.

- Objective: Increase the number of repeat buyers of Product X by 25 percent.

In this case, the objective does not support the goal. The goal is about *new* customers and the objective talks about *existing* customers. An objective that would be aligned, or relevant, in this case might be: Increase the number of new buyers in the XYZ market area by 25 percent. That is an objective that would serve to meet the goal of expanding market share.

3.5 Objectives must be time bound

One element that all of the previous examples are missing — and it's an important element — is a time frame. "Time bound" simply means that there needs to be some indication of when the objective is expected to be achieved. By what date or during what time frame? If you start your objective as: "Increase the number of repeat buyers of Product X by 25 percent," but don't indicate when that objective should be achieved, at the end of the year when you examine the results and they are only at 20 percent, a team member or the marketing manager could legitimately say, "I was thinking we'd do this by the end of *next* year!"

Well-developed objectives help you keep your team on track in terms of what the intended outcomes are, so that at the end of the time line you've established, two or more independent observers can say "Yes, we did" or "No, we didn't" achieve this objective.

3.6 Evaluating your objectives

In addition to reviewing each objective and holding it up to the SMART criteria, you should also consider the overall objectives that you've established under each of your goals and ask the following questions:

- Will these objectives be sufficient to achieve the identified goal (or goals)?

- Do we have the resources we'll need to accomplish the objectives?

- Are the time frames we've established appropriate for achieving the stated objectives?

4. The Importance of Objectives

We've already talked about the importance of well-developed direct mail objectives in terms of allowing you to determine whether or not you've achieved success and to ensure that two or more independent observers can reach the same conclusion based on the way the objectives have been stated. That is very important.

Equally if not more important is the role that objectives play in helping to provide a framework or point of reference for all the planning activities and steps that will be undertaken to develop and implement your direct mail campaign. Your objectives will serve as a guide or checkpoint as you create your offer, select lists, develop copy and design, and deploy your campaign. At each point along the way you should ask:

- Does this activity or decision support our stated objective?

- Is this activity or decision likely to help us achieve our stated objective?

If the answers are "no," the activity should be modified or the decision changed.

Once you have your goals and objectives established, the next step in developing your direct mail campaign is to consider your target audience or audiences. As you'll see, the more specific and precise you can be about your target audience, the better you'll be able to make effective list choices (a critical part of direct mail marketing) and create communications aimed at achieving the results you want.

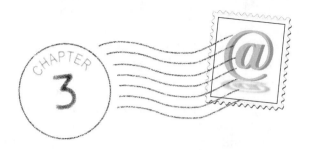

Targeting Your Market

Direct mail has many benefits as we've already seen. One of them is the ability to target niche market segments that can represent very specific groups of people based on their demographics, psychographics, and even purchasing habits. Even in a mass-media market that has become increasingly segmented, advertisers have significant "waste" in terms of the people they're reaching with their advertising messages who simply are not interested in what they have to offer. With direct mail — both traditional and email — marketers can be much more precise in targeting consumers who are most likely to be interested in what they have to offer. This presumes, of course, that they have taken the time to seriously and carefully consider who their target audience is.

1. Identify Your Target Audience

Once you thoroughly understand what it is you're trying to sell, you can turn to the question of who you are trying to sell it to and how best to reach them. Consider these questions:

- Who are you trying to reach?
- When do you want to reach these customers?
- Where do your prospects live?
- How often do you want to reach potential customers?

Direct mail can be used to target both prospects and existing customers in creative ways. The key is to clearly identify the characteristics that potential customers have, based on your own analysis, past purchase history, and any secondary purchasing information you can attain. The following examples demonstrate businesses targeting their markets:

- iSchool Music & Art is an educational music and art school for children and adults in Port Washington and Syosset, Long Island, NY. With a goal of increasing new student enrollment and recognizing that its real target audience was *parents* of students (many who begin considering educational options for their children when they're quite young), the school targeted residences in multiple zip codes representing the areas its students typically come from with children aged 3 to 17 years old. "We will typically enroll about 100 new students at each location from each mailing," the school says.

- Texoma Community Credit Union wanted to generate CDs (Certificates of Deposit, a type of term deposit), and decided to promote a great interest rate on CDs to 2,400 homeowner-investors from a rented list as well as its own existing top depositors. The promotion generated 198 CDs representing $5.31 million in new investments for the credit union.

- Verlo Mattress promoted a ten-day sale through a direct mail effort using postcards that were sent to a list comprised of its own customers who had purchased directly from its stores over the past two years, and customers who had purchased from Verlo Mattress stores that had closed within the past three years but who were near enough to consider shopping at its locations. The result: $56,000 in sales.

When considering who to target, you should ask yourself the following questions:

- **Who are you trying to reach?** Define your potential customers in terms of both demographic and psychographic characteristics. Demographic characteristics include such things as age, gender, income, education, family status, and occupation. Psychographic characteristics involve lifestyle or attitudes. If you don't know specifically who you're trying to reach, you'll have a very difficult time trying to determine the best list to use, and whether it's best to reach out through the mail or online media.

- **When do you want to reach these customers?** If your product is seasonal such as snowboarding equipment, you will not be mailing in mid-July. Be careful, however, not to reach your customers too late. Your goal is to reach the consumer at the time the purchasing decision is made — this is not necessarily the same point at which the purchase is made. You may very well find that you need to begin promoting snowboarding gear in late September or early October.

- **Where do your prospects live?** Your choice of list will certainly depend on where your prospects live. Perhaps your product has national appeal and you are able to use national lists. However, again, the beauty of direct mail is that it can be precise. You may want to more narrowly segment your audience by region of the country, size of the city, etc. Or, you may be marketing internationally, which expands your options considerably.

- **How often do you want to reach your prospects?** Will you do regular monthly mailings? Quarterly? It's important to mail your own customer list on a regular basis so you keep your name before them and take advantage of the momentum created by any recent purchases. You'll want to monitor the responses to these mailings closely to ensure you aren't mailing either too often or too infrequently.

- **Where do you want to reach potential customers?** At home? In the office? The type of product or service you provide will determine the best place for reaching prospects. If you are selling a subscription to a trade publication, you would most likely want to reach prospects in the office. If you are selling clothing, you probably want to reach them at home. However, this isn't always the case. You may want to test some different approaches just to see what kind of response you get.

Once you've thoroughly analyzed your customers, you need to take a close look at your prospects. To whom are you trying to sell your product? The following questions can help you get a good feel for your audience:

- Are your best prospects men or women?

- Are they young, middle-aged, or retirees?

- What is their average annual income?

- Where do they live?

- What do they like to do in their spare time?

- How much do they already know about the product or service you have to offer?

Reviewing the information you have about your existing customers can help you develop a profile that can be used to find more people like them who will, presumably, also be interested in your product or service. It's extremely important to know who your current customers are. By knowing the characteristics of current customers, you'll have a much easier time of prospecting for new customers because you'll know exactly what to look for when you're researching mailing list availability. If you don't have all of this information, you may want to consider conducting some research or getting access to secondary sources that can provide you with important insights and information. Secondary sources may include research or information available through trade organizations that serve the market you're interested in, or data available through the US Government (e.g., the Census Bureau).

1.1 Identify your target market's buying habits

Another important aspect of identifying your market is determining their specific buying habits. When you're considering the purchasing habits of your potential customers, you'll want to know the following information regarding the product you're selling:

- **Where do customers typically buy this product?** Suppose you're introducing a line of deli foods that you'd like to sell through the mail. Traditionally, customers would buy deli items at a deli. You'll need to address this obvious objection to purchasing through the mail in your advertising materials. In addition, knowing that there are alternative sources of supply will help you in determining pricing, developing unique benefits, and structuring your offer.

- **Are purchases seasonal or special occasion?** The answer to this question will help you plan your mailing strategy. Obviously, if you're selling Christmas items, you won't be mailing in June; neither would you mail in December, which would be too far into the holiday season. You might, instead, opt for a late October mailing date. Seasonal considerations also apply to swimwear, educational materials (which often see low sales during the summer months), and gardening supplies.

- **Is purchase premeditated or impulsive?** Direct mail works best for selling impulse items. Premeditated purchases (e.g., cars) lead consumers to local retail outlets. They don't sit around to wait for a brochure to show up in their mailbox.

- **How does your price compare with competitors?** Pricing is a major consideration, as it forms the basis for your offer. Know who your competitors are — both your direct mail competitors and alternative sources of supply. If a consumer can conveniently buy a very similar item locally at a good price, your direct mail offer may not have much appeal. You'll need to structure an offer that points out the benefits of your pricing, fast delivery, etc., to woo them from more traditional sources of supply.

2. Segmenting, Targeting, and Positioning

Once you have a good general idea of the consumers you wish to reach, it's a good idea to get more specific. Segmenting, targeting, and positioning are three key terms in marketing that apply to direct mail marketing efforts.

2.1 Segmentation

Segmenting involves breaking the consumer universe down into manageable market segments. The goal is to reach the most highly responsive consumers at the least cost. There are an infinite number of segments that an organization might choose for its marketing efforts, and various ways in which segmentation may be approached.

Demographic segmentation, for example, breaks the market down in terms of various demographic characteristics such as age, gender, race, marital status, income, education, and occupation.

Psychographic segmentation, by contrast, breaks the market down in terms of activities, interests, and opinions (AIO). An example of psychographic segmentation would be a sports retailer appealing to individuals who enjoy rock climbing.

For market segmentation to be effective, Charles D. Schewe and Alexander Hiam, authors of *The Portable MBA in Marketing*, suggest certain criteria must be met. They include:

- The market must be identifiable and measurable. Segmentation needs to be based on some shared characteristic (e.g., enjoying country music or being a teenager).

- The segment must be large enough to be profitable.

- The market must be reachable. Marketers can reach females between the ages of 25 to 40 without much trouble, but attempting to reach 15-year-old redheaded boys or mothers of lactose intolerant children who enjoy cooking will be more challenging.

- The segment must be responsive. Young women in their early twenties might be a promising segment for a high-end hair product, but not if they're in college and struggling to pay rent and tuition.

- The segment must not be expected to change quickly.

Segmentation may also be based on internal information. Usage patterns may suggest certain segments of customers who are more responsive (e.g., heavy users of a particular product). There are infinite possibilities involved in identifying market segments, as segments may be comprised of psychographic, demographic, and usage criteria in various combinations. Once these possibilities have been identified, the next step for the marketer is to determine which segments to target.

2.2 Targeting

The goal for marketers once segments have been selected is to prioritize those that are likely to be most responsive. Competition is an important factor in considering which segments to focus on. If a major competitor has already chosen a particular market segment, that segment might not be as promising to you as another segment that has not yet been selected by the competition.

Consequently, when considering which specific market segments to target, it is important to consider the activities of the competition — both direct and indirect competitors.

Direct competitors are fairly obvious. Target is a direct competitor for Walmart. Red Lobster is a direct competitor for Outback Steakhouse. Indirect competition can be more difficult to identify and is sometimes overlooked as a consideration.

Indirect competitors represent alternatives to your product. For instance, indirect competition for Target and Walmart could be a wide range of other stores, both brick and mortar and online. Local grocery stores (or eating at home) represent indirect competition for both Red Lobster and Outback Steakhouse.

Thoroughly understanding the competition for your products and services — direct and indirect — can help you to be more precise in targeting specific segments that are most likely to respond to what you have to offer. You will want to target those segments where you believe you can have the most impact because the attributes of your products or service (e.g., quality, price, service, etc.) are competitive when compared to these other options.

Keep in mind, though, that the segment that offers the most in terms of numbers of potential customers is not necessarily the segment you should select. These obvious segments have most likely already been targeted by your competitors. Your best opportunities may be in smaller segments that have not yet been pursued by others — even though the numbers may be smaller, the potential for positive impact will be greater.

2.3 Positioning

According to the American Marketing Association, "positioning refers to the customer's perceptions of the place a product or brand occupies in a market segment." In some markets, a position is achieved by associating the benefits of a brand with the needs or lifestyle of the segments. More often, positioning involves the differentiation of the company's offering from the competition by making or implying a comparison in terms of specific attributes.

Walmart has positioned itself as the low price leader. Its positioning statement prominently displayed on its website and in communication materials includes the statement: "Always low prices. Always." Contrast this position with that of Nordstrom, which states that "the company's philosophy has remained unchanged for more than 100 years since its establishment by John W. Nordstrom in 1901: offer the customer the best possible service, selection, quality, and value." Nordstrom has selected a position based on service, selection, quality, and value — not price. Subtly different, yet clearly apparent to consumers who have shopped at both stores.

Your company may already have a stated mission and perhaps even an established segmenting, targeting, and positioning strategy in place. Even so, it's important to revisit your statements and strategies regularly to ensure they are still relevant and appropriate.

3. Your USP — Unique Selling Proposition

Another important consideration in marketing is what is known as a "unique selling proposition" or USP. A USP represents something about your product or service that is different from competing products and services in important ways which represent value for your potential customers. It's what makes you not only different, but *valued*. Clarifying your USP can help you establish a strong position in your marketplace and can also serve as the basis for the direct mail messages (words and images) that you will eventually create.

Your USP conveys those qualities that are *unique* in that they are about what you have to offer; something that none of your competitors have to offer. *Selling* in that it's a benefit — something that will appeal to a potential customer. *Proposition* in that it's an offer you're making to people who buy your product. After all, if your product is just like all the rest, why would anybody choose you? There has to be something that sets you apart from the crowd. That something can be as simple as a good location or a low price. Or, it can be as complex as a refined manufacturing technique that allows your product to literally last forever.

What does your company's product or service offer that nobody else has, or that very few others have to offer? Do you give a full money-back guarantee? Does your product experience extend back many years? Do you offer free maintenance? Do customers receive an add-on gift for making a purchase? Does your product differ in some integral way from your competitors' products?

In some cases, your USP may be very apparent. In other cases, you may need to spend a great deal of time thinking of a slant that's effective and appropriate. Maybe, as in the case of Maytag and their "lonely" repair staff, your USP is more a subjective image than a hard fact. The point is that once you've developed a USP, you have a hook that can help you grab the customer, but only if you use it effectively in your communication materials.

Your USP allows you to create awareness of your product or service by differentiating it from similar products or services available to your customers. Once you've established what your unique selling proposition is, you need to make sure that it plays an integral role in any marketing communication you do.

To identify a USP, you need to consider the following:

- Which product or service benefits are *most* important to your target market?

- Which benefits do you "own" (i.e., benefits not already claimed by your competitors and not easily imitated by your competitors)?

- Which benefits will be most easily understood by your target audience?

The resulting statement should be a one-line statement that contains a clearly identifiable, unique benefit that is meaningful to your market. Do you remember the following?

- Wonder Bread: "Helps build strong bodies 12 ways."

- KFC: "It's finger-lickin' good."

- Burger King: "Have it your way."

Note that in each of these statements it is not the literal translation of the words, but the overall impact of the benefit implied in each statement that makes the USP truly powerful. That is the challenge that marketing communicators should embrace when working toward the development of copy that will achieve results.

Note, also, that each of these statements *could* have been made by the competition in each product category. The power of an effective USP is that it can create the *perception* of uniqueness in the mind of consumers.

Once you've developed a USP, it should be implicit in all of your direct mail (and other marketing communications) materials.

4. Is Your Target Market Online?

An important audience consideration in this digital age is whether or not your target market is online. Despite the fact that the Internet, social media, and online marketing seem to be what "everybody who is anybody" is talking about these days, marketers should not assume that they should be attempting to reach their audience online. It depends. Just as when researching and analyzing other attributes about your potential audience (e.g., age, income, geography), you need to consider whether your target market may be effectively reached online or whether they are still best reached through traditional mail.

General research can provide some direction. For instance, Pew Research Center conducted a survey in 2010[1] which surprisingly

---

[1] Pew Research Center's Home Broadband 2010 survey: www.pewinternet.org/~/media//Files/Reports/2010/Home broadband 2010.pdf. Accessed March 18, 2011.

points out that about one-third of the American population does not use a broadband (Internet) connection in their homes. Two-thirds (66 percent) of American adults do currently use a high-speed Internet connection at home, up only 3 percent since the 2009 survey. There are racial differences, as well. For instance, broadband adoption by African-Americans now stands at 56 percent, up from 46 percent in 2009. Clearly not everybody uses the Internet. Therefore, it is very important for marketers to find out whether *their* target audiences are among the two-thirds who indicate they do use high-speed Internet in their homes. Data also suggests that a significant amount of nonbusiness Internet use occurs in the workplace.

Here's what some consumers had to say about the issue:

- "Snail mail can be useful. It has the 'different' factor. A well-written, handwritten note from an advertiser can go a long way toward creating consumer interest ... if it has the differentiating factor. It may be a bit tedious to create, but the effect will last longer. Too often email is considered spam and deleted without opening."

- "Direct mail if well-presented would lead to it being opened. The fact is, direct mail has a higher rate of being opened than email. With the latter, it's just so easy to trash it, but when people hold it in their hand and are either walking into the house or the office, they have time to spare and would likely be opening the mail. So, old-fashioned mail is better to me."

- "Probably snail mail gets more attention — first because there's less of it. Second, because it takes fractionally longer to dispose of. I actually have to walk with it to a waste paper bin to drop it in so it has a few seconds to engage my attention. Third, because the physical medium allows a variety of shapes, sizes, even feel of paper and a bulge which just might be a freebie inside that I might be interested in. All email has is bold type in the subject line to get my attention. Fourth, and last, because there's always a chance that it might be something useful. Most snail mail gets read, whereas with email they're often just dropped in the trash."

Are these comments reflective of your target audience? Who knows? The point is don't assume, either one way or the other. If you don't know your consumers well enough to determine whether traditional direct mail, the online variety, or a combination of both would be most effective, it certainly pays to find out!

5. Structuring Your Offer to Get Results

In direct mail, it's all about getting to the point. What is it you want the consumer to do? In short, what's the offer? The offer is so important in direct mail that many marketers start here first. It makes sense. Before you can adequately begin framing your pitch you need to know what it is you're trying to sell. In other words, what do you have to offer?

There are a number of different types of offers, including cash in advance ("refund if you're not completely satisfied") and negative option ("I agree to review future shipments and understand that I can return them in X days if I decide not to keep them").

Some offers are very simple: "Buy this backpack for only $9.99." Others are more complex: "Buy this backpack for only $9.99 when you sign up for our DVD-of-the-month club. You'll automatically be sent our selection of the month every 30 days. You'll have 10 days to review the shipment and keep or return it. In addition, you can always select from among the titles in our member catalog. Choose any selection for only $14.99. After you've made 3 purchases during your first year of membership, you'll be eligible for even greater savings!"

The structuring of an offer is an important step in developing your direct mail package. The wrong offer can make your entire mailing fall flat; the right one can make it soar.

Even the simplest offer can be presented in a number of different ways. What you have to offer is a bit more nuanced than "Buy my widgets!" Your challenge, as a direct marketer, is to select the way that will be most appealing to your customer. The following are a number of different offer options you might want to consider:

- **By invitation only.** This can lend an aura of exclusivity to your offer and is particularly effective when used in mailings to your customer list. For example, "Since you purchased from us in the past, we'd like to offer you this new product at a 25% discount. This offer is only available to past customers."

- **Limited time.** You can create a sense of urgency by limiting your offer. "Respond by January 1 to take advantage of this special price," or "Quantities limited, order now!" are just two of the ways you could structure a limited time offer.

- **Get there first or limited supply.** This type of offer creates a sense of urgency and may give prospects that extra push they need to make a buying decision. For instance, "Free widget to the first 100 people to order." Do you carefully police the number of people who get the free widget? Of course not. By sending a free widget with every order (for a reasonable period of time), you'll be creating good will with all of your customers because each will feel that they won.

- **Free gift.** The free gift or premium offer is very common. You've probably seen this type of offer for magazine subscriptions, mobile phone plans, etc. What kind of gift should you offer? The best is one which is related somehow to the product itself. For example, if you're selling women's clothing, you might offer a free piece of jewelry. If you're selling a training program on DVD, you might offer a free whitepaper of tips related to the topic of the program.

- **Discounts.** An offer of a discount can be structured in a number of ways, such as "Buy one, get one free," or "Half-price sale." Be careful, though, that you don't use discounts too often. There are two reasons for this:

  Offering discounts makes a statement about your product. A product which can never be purchased at a discount acquires a certain status.

  Customers can become accustomed to receiving discounts from you if you do it too regularly. They may come to look at your discounted prices as your "regular" prices and the effectiveness of the offers will wane.

- **Quantity discounts.** When creating quantity discounts, carefully consider where to place your price breaks. Don't make the first break too large. You want to choose a point where it will be easy for the customer to say: "Oh, what the heck, if I add $5 more to my order, I'll get $x off." Effective quantity discounts can help you to dramatically increase your average order size. For instance, "Take a 10% discount when you buy 10, a 20% discount when you buy 20." "On orders more than $100, we'll take $10 off." "Call about quantity discounts for bulk purchases."

- **Cost per week.** You've probably seen this technique often with advertisements for magazines: "Only 43 cents a week will bring you timely issues of *Our Magazine*!" Breaking down the price of your product can be especially effective if you're selling a high-ticket item with a price that might put off prospects. Framing it in a weekly or even monthly time line can make the purchase decision less risky.

- **Free examination.** The easier you can make it for your customer to order, the more likely you are to get the order. How much easier could it be than to simply check a box and toss a business reply card into the mail? If you decide to use this technique, monitor your returns and all the costs associated with those returns and the order processing very carefully. With a strong product, this technique can work very well. With a marginal product, you may find that the costs of handling returns (and your final back-end results) don't justify a "send no money now" offer. Note that the final back-end results are the overall results of the campaign after returns have been taken into consideration. In other words, you can't just consider the overall number of orders that have been received; you also need to take into consideration any returns so that you have an accurate reflection of the results.

- **Free trial.** The free trial offer is a good way to get your product into the hands of your customers, and because it's "free," response can be increased. For example, "Try our product for 30 days. If it doesn't do everything we say it will do, send it back. You'll owe nothing." As with the free examination offer mentioned in the point above, back-end results must be monitored very carefully.

- **Money-back guarantee.** Minimize risks for your customers by offering a generous guarantee — ordering through the mail, or online, can be risky. The customers haven't seen the product and have only your copy and graphics, perhaps a photo, to judge the value of their purchase. If they aren't given a guarantee of their satisfaction, they may decide that the risk of ordering is too high. In direct mail, guarantees are a must. They are by far the most important part of your offer. Don't neglect to include one.

- **Special offers for new customers.** We've all been on the receiving end of an offer inviting us to become a new customer of some business or other and promising us a great discount or enticing bonus to do so. That's great if we're a new customer. But what if we're an *existing* customer? What's in it for us? While offers like this can certainly be effective in attracting new business, marketers need to be cautious that in the process of wooing new customers they don't inadvertently upset their existing loyal customers.

- **Last chance offers.** A last chance offer attempts to prompt a purchase from respondents who may be motivated by the thought that they won't have another opportunity to buy. This can be effective, but only if the last chance is real. We can all think of organizations that use the "going out of business" sale over and over again. Eventually, the effectiveness of this technique, and the credibility of the organization, will suffer.

- **Varying payment options.** Marketers may use a variety of payment options to influence the purchase decision. By offering quantity discounts, for instance, marketers may be able to sell more of a particular product than they might have sold at a single unit price. Consumers will feel as though they are getting a special deal and may be prompted to add on "just one more" item. This concept is quite common online, where retailers will offer free shipping for purchases over a certain dollar amount. Consumers may spend more than they might have otherwise to take advantage of the free shipping — even when the shipping costs may be less than the additional purchase.

Which offer will work best for you? It depends on a lot of things — your product and your market, for starters. Direct mail is once again beneficial here because we can test offers to determine what might work best for us.

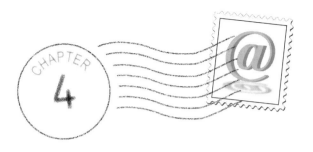

Lists

The mailing list is a critical element of a successful direct mail program. The list represents your market, and is the aspect of this form of marketing which makes it so *direct*. Unlike other forms of mass-media advertising, you are specifically targeting individuals who for some reason you believe will have an interest in your product or service. There is little wasted effort in terms of sending your message to people who have no interest whatsoever in what you have to offer. Your goal is to find that perfect audience that most clearly represents people who are going to raise their hands and say, "Yes, we want to order that!"

There have traditionally been two options when it comes to obtaining lists for your direct mail marketing efforts:

1. Compile a list.

2. Rent or purchase a list.

The digital world has introduced a third option — co-registration (see section **3.1** for more details).

To those who are newly introduced to direct mail, the concept of mailing lists can be a heady discovery. A mailing list is simply a list of names and addresses (snail mail or email) of businesses or individuals. This basic information can be enhanced with other bits of data that are added to the record. For instance, one label on a traditional direct mail list to be used through the US Postal Service might look like this:

John Doe
1792 N. Highland Ave.
Chicago, IL 60410

Within the computer where that record was stored, though, there is likely to exist a lot of other details about John. If this name was provided by a company that John did business with, it could have a list of items he purchased, the dates he purchased them, and how much he paid. The company probably also has his telephone number and, increasingly, his email address. It may also have his age, his occupation, his household income, and any number of other important details about John.

Database management systems make it possible to gather and maintain amazing amounts of data on individuals and organizations. Databases can be appended with additional information from other sources to provide even greater detail about customers and prospects. All of this information allows marketers to be very particular when using their own lists, or renting or purchasing someone else's list.

1. Compiling Lists — Your Prospect and Customer Database

Whether you have 10 or 10,000 customers, your mailing list is a valuable commodity. Are you making the best use of your customer file? Consider the following questions:

- Do you know who your past customers are?

- Do you make use of follow-up sales promotions?

- Do you keep an active prospect list?

- Do you have a means of identifying recent purchases and customers of specific products?

Every business has two major categories of lists — a prospect list and a customer list. Each is a valuable commodity, but each needs to be managed in a slightly different way.

Maintenance of your *customer* list involves adding customer names, updating addresses and other information, and deleting names of people who have not been customers for a certain period of time. One of the big questions you will need to ask yourself as you begin to build a customer database is, "What information do I want to keep on each customer?" The answer depends on both your marketing approach and on the capability of your database management system. At a bare minimum, you will want the following information about your current customers:

- Full name

- Address

- Phone numbers (home, work, mobile)

- Email address

- Purchase history (including both an itemization of what they have purchased from you in the past and the date of each purchase)

Your *prospect* list is a list of those people who you feel *may* become customers. You may feel this way because they've expressed an interest in your products or services, because they've visited your website and shared their contact information, because they've been referred to you by a current customer, or because you know they have interests that indicate they may be potential customers. The type of information you'll want about your prospects includes:

- Full name

- Address

- Phone numbers (home, work, mobile)

- How they were added to your list

- When they were added to your list

When your business is small, it can be easy to keep track of your customers and prospects through programs such as Microsoft Excel or QuickBooks. As your business and lists grow, you will find that you can benefit from more functionality and more sophistication in terms of how you manage your database. Microsoft Access is a database program that can provide additional functionality and many small businesses use it quite effectively. Others turn to even more powerful options offered by companies such as Salesforce.com or Infusionsoft.

1.1 Database marketing and Customer Relationship Management (CRM)

Today, if you're involved in direct mail, you've probably heard about the power and flexibility of a well-designed, accurate, and up-to-date database. There is an abundance of available literature on database marketing and it's a topic that's covered at literally every direct mail conference held. Unfortunately, it's a concept that's sometimes shrouded in unnecessary mystery.

Database marketing is a relatively simple marketing concept. In fact, many direct marketers already operate a database marketing system of sorts. However, the mere creation of a database doesn't automatically launch you into the world of database marketing. Before you can do that you need to develop an organized system for managing all that data. This means coming up with ways to organize it, update and maintain it, and retrieve and manipulate information from it.

A database is nothing more than a collection of data about a group of related "things." When we're discussing database development, these "things" will be your customers or prospects. The data you're collecting will include much more than simply the names and addresses of the customers. All of the information you maintain on your customers will be in your database, and because of the way you've collected that data, you'll be able to retrieve it in the form of mailing lists, management reports, billing statements, etc. A database is built over time. You'll test it, expand it, and rearrange it until you find a system that is as flexible and efficient as you need it to be.

The larger your customer base or the more complex your products and services, the more likely that setting up a customer database will be appropriate for you. Database marketing has a number of benefits to offer:

- Increased productivity. You'll save time by automating many of the tasks that you currently handle manually (e.g., generation of mailing lists, preparation of sales reports, various accounting functions).

- Quick retrieval of names and addresses sorted by various finite characteristics.

- Automated generation of commonly used business forms (e.g., invoices, statements, form letters, accounting reports).

- Collection and analysis of marketing information (speedy information on such things as how many customers purchased the XYZ product at $X versus $Y, or how many customers have purchased five or more items from your business).

By maintaining a database you will be able to describe your customer list in terms of recency, frequency, value, type of product purchased, or any other characteristic you choose to collect, enter, and maintain. This is valuable marketing information that even some of the smallest companies can take advantage of in one form or another.

The importance of this information can be quickly and easily demonstrated through cross-selling. Cross-selling in this context involves selling an item to a customer who has purchased a similar item in the past.

Suppose you market seminars. You recently developed an advanced ceramics seminar as a follow-up to your basic ceramics program. With your database, you will be able to easily request a list of all these people who attended your basic ceramics class. You can then do a special mailing to these people telling them about your upcoming advanced course. You not only save money by not mailing *all* of the customers on your list, but you're able to prepare a very personalized mailing that is guaranteed to get a better response than a general program announcement would.

Perhaps one of the most interesting applications of database marketing is the ability to profile your customers. Depending on the information you maintain, you will be able to eventually put together a typical customer profile that will aid you immeasurably as you go out and prospect for new customers. For instance, your database tells you that your typical customer is female, between the ages of 35 to 45, married with two children, and her typical purchases are household items between $15 and $35.

The benefits of your database are virtually limitless, but these benefits are dependent on your creativity, forethought, and organization. Remember, what you put in is what you'll be able to get out. No more.

1.2 Deciding what data to keep

Before you can even begin to set up a database you need to thoroughly examine your needs. Put these needs in writing and be as specific as possible, but don't attempt to take this task on by yourself. Ask for input. Don't design your database in a vacuum. The kind of input you need to develop a successful database can come from three important sources:

- Other people who will need to access the database (e.g., clerical support, accounting personnel, etc.)

- Other people who will rely on your output to perform their jobs (e.g., a mailing house that wants labels to be printed in a specific way)

- Other people who have developed databases of their own and can warn you about potential pitfalls and make helpful, time-saving suggestions based on their own experiences

Spend some time speaking with these people; ask for their opinions of what they would like the database to be able to do and what type of information they think you should collect. Of course, there's no end to the amount of information you *could* store in your database. As always, though, financial considerations come into play. You need to be able to separate "nice to know" from "need to know."

For example, if you're running a mail-order business, you *need* to know the addresses of your customers and you also *need* to know what their purchase histories are. It might be *nice* to know some demographic information about these customers (e.g., birthdates, the number of people in their households). However, the cost of gathering, inputting, and maintaining this information might not make it worth your while to capture it in the first place. These are the kinds of decisions you will have to make for yourself based upon your budget and your anticipated marketing goals. Here are some standard items that are often included in customer databases:

- Name, address, telephone, and email address

- Website address

- Social media contact info

- Purchase history (including types of purchases, dates of purchases, units purchased, monetary value of purchases)

- Source of sale (e.g., response to a direct mail brochure, response to a space advertisement, word of mouth, direct salesperson, retail outlet)

- Credit information

- Type of purchase (sports clothing versus formal apparel, for instance)

You might also decide to set up an inquiry file, a prospect file, or a gift-recipient file in addition to your actual customer file. These names would be prospects for future sales even though they have not personally purchased from you in the past.

1.3 Using databases for mailing maximization

Employing technology is a huge change over the past several years when it comes to direct mailing efficiencies. The use of databases can help marketers select customers based on a variety of data elements representing demographic as well as purchasing data. Databases can be analyzed to help profile and identify new potential customers direct marketers can then reach out to. The concept isn't new. Direct marketers have been doing this type of analysis since the beginning of direct marketing; what's new is the technology that allows the process to be automated.

Mining existing data can help identify opportunities and trends. The resulting analytics, when used strategically, can direct future activities to high-priority efforts that can make a bigger difference. Existing information can be used to profile current customers and prospects. Those profiles can then be used to reach out to the surrounding market to find others with the same or similar profiles. Existing data can also be augmented through the use of external sources that can be appended and can provide additional intelligence about customers which can help direct marketing and sales efforts.

Once commonly referred to as "data mining," the practice of using data to direct strategic marketing decisions is now becoming known as "analytics," which is a practice that is showing great promise for companies large and small. While the systems available are increasingly sophisticated and offer ample opportunities for direct marketers hoping to make better use of the masses of data available to them, even small companies and entrepreneurs that may not be able to invest in large systems or expensive software packages can use analytics to make sound decisions.

Even gathering the information doesn't have to be a major undertaking involving the purchase of data from external sources. Companies can survey their customers or target markets to gather information. That data can then be used to draw conclusions based on a particular sector, industry, or size.

1.4 Internal versus external — factors to consider

It's not always necessary to maintain your database on your premises, and for the small-business owner, it's often not possible. It can certainly be less expensive to use an outside service bureau than to build and maintain your own system. Software as a Service (SaaS) and a rapidly expanding cloud computing environment also means that you can easily take advantage of various technological options for maintaining your lists in secure environments that you can access from literally anywhere, and at a fraction of the cost of managing your own hardware and software infrastructures. Add to that the benefit of leveraging the expertise of major players in the fields of security, privacy, and other risk-management-related issues, and it's easy to see how external hosting can make sense.

1.5 Pitfalls to avoid

There are a number of pitfalls to avoid as you contemplate the development of a database marketing system. First and foremost is failing to gather enough information in advance. The importance of good communication cannot be emphasized enough. Make sure that you know what your needs are now and have a good idea of what your needs may be in the future. Make sure that everyone who will be using the system for information, for work output, or for data entry, has had the opportunity for input. Make sure you develop a system that can coordinate all the varied needs of your company into an efficiently operating database.

The second most important pitfall to avoid is sloppy maintenance of information. The information you pull from your database will lose its value quickly if it's incorrectly entered or sloppily maintained. It's a good idea to establish a detailed order entry manual for your company which includes standards of address entry and address corrections, and what to do in the event of certain specific situations (e.g., wrong price, use of PO box versus street address, storage and maintenance of "shipped to" versus "billed" name and address). Consistency is important — remember the old computer motto: "garbage in, garbage out." Take steps to ensure that no garbage is going into your database.

Here are some additional pitfalls to avoid:

- Data fields which are too small, especially in the name and address areas.

- Data that is not maintained in separate fields. One company combined first and last names into one field and later found that it would be impossible to send out personalized letters to customers which read "Dear John" instead of "Dear John Smith."

- No allowance for changes in the future. Don't paint yourself into a corner with your database. For example, make sure that you've left flexibility for the addition of fields at a later date.

Some additional tips:

- Capture names whenever and wherever you can. Names mean money. Every time you can add a name to your list, whether it's a customer name or a prospect name, you're adding the potential for a future sale.

- If you offer webinars, white papers, or other free stuff as a way of increasing business, make sure you're capturing and keeping contact information from everyone who responds — whether or not they actually follow through with completing the event.

- Whenever you make a sale, ask for the customer's name, address, phone number, and email address. Make this part of your procedure for issuing a sales receipt. If the customer writes a check, you can get the information you need directly from that check.

- Have a box and sign placed prominently in your store (if you have a physical location) where browsers can easily see it. Have the sign say something like, "We're constantly adding new products and/or offering new courses. Would you like to be on our mailing list? Please fill out one of the forms beside this box." These names can be added to your prospect list.

- Ask for referrals. Offer special gifts to customers who can get a friend to join your mailing list or shop at your store. You've now got a new customer to add to your list.

- Mail to your customers regularly. "Your best customers are your best customers." This may seem like a silly statement, but it's true. You need to keep your customers loyal. One way of doing this is by constantly reminding them that you're still around!

- Take advantage of every opportunity to promote new products and services to customers who have made similar purchases in the past. This type of promotion is one of the most effective for any direct marketer.

- Keep your list clean. You should schedule a regular (perhaps semiannual) mailing to customers who haven't been active for X months. The mailing could be on the order of, "We want you back ... if we don't hear from you by X date, we'll be forced to remove your name from our mailing list." Remove the names of nonrespondents and update the history of those who *do* respond.

2. Renting and Purchasing Lists

While developing and maintaining your own list is extremely important for your direct mail efforts, using lists from other sources can help you expand both your prospect and your customer files! Renting names is big business and has been for many years. EdithRoman (www.edithroman.com) has been engaged in list rental for more than 50 years.

SRDS Media Solutions, a source of information on the availability of lists (as well as rates for the broad range of media outlets), was founded in 1919! Formerly known as Standard Rate and Data Service, SRDS (now available online) remains a leading source of information on the availability of literally thousands of consumer and business lists.

Anyone who compiles a list is a list owner, and many list owners choose to rent their lists to other marketers. List owners represent both business people like you who offer their own customer lists and list compilers who put together lists from various sources and make them available to marketers. For instance, many companies compile their lists directly from telephone directories or voter registration lists. It's virtually impossible for anyone to stay off of these lists and most people are on multiple lists. In fact, the closest you can come to having your name removed from these lists and trying to minimize the clutter that may accrue in your mailbox (the old-fashioned kind and online) is to contact the Direct Marketing Association and ask that your name be placed on their Mail Preference Service list. This is a service whereby consumers who do not wish to receive mail advertising can request that their names be removed from a large number of mailing lists. However, since companies are not required to participate in this service, even taking this step will not ensure that you will no longer receive any unsolicited postal mail.

If you're curious about how a simple purchase decision can lead to offers from a wide range of marketers, you can do this: reply to a direct mail solicitation using a slight variation of your name (with traditional direct mail) or an email account set up with a unique name, and then watch to see what you begin receiving in that name. It's an interesting exercise and one that can help you become familiar with the fast-paced nature of the mailing industry.

2.1 Find a list broker

Where do you get lists? From list brokers. Yes, lists are such big business that there are a lot of people who have set up companies for the sole purpose of renting out lists. Why? Because there are millions of names that can be listed in an infinite variety of ways. While you can attempt to research the list market yourself and order directly from the list source (e.g., magazine publisher), it's much simpler to use a list broker. The list broker will coordinate all of the necessary arrangements for ordering your lists, help you with list research, and make recommendations to you on list selections. The broker can also provide you with countless tips and inside information that you would not have been able to find on your own.

List brokers make their money by charging a commission to the person renting the list. A magazine publisher, for example, might charge $80/m (m = thousand) for a list. The broker would get a percentage of that amount for their work on the account. Considering that many large companies mail to many millions of names each year, you can easily see why renting lists is big business.

When working with a broker it's important to make sure that the broker thoroughly understands your business, your market, and what you're trying to accomplish. Many brokers are specialists whose knowledge of your particular business may be minimal if your business is not one the broker specializes in. If that's the case, you may find that the information you're getting from your broker is no more detailed than what you could find yourself.

Your broker should be like a partner in your business. The broker needs to know what you're selling, who your market is, what your promotional mailings are like, and ultimately, how well each of your mailings is working. If you don't provide this information, you won't be getting the quality of service that can help boost your responses.

You shouldn't have to be a large mailer to get quality attention from list brokers. A good broker will realize that your business has potential for growth in the future and will want to work with you now even though your orders may be small. Why? Because that broker is hoping that, as your needs grow, you'll continue to rely on the same service you got when you were starting out.

2.2 Types of lists

There are different types of lists that you may want to consider, such as consumer, response, and business lists.

Consumer lists are lists of consumers (potential customers) that may be either compiled or response lists. Compiled lists are lists of people drawn from various sources such as Yellow Pages listings, drivers' license records, census data, etc. There are various ways these lists can be segmented to narrow the number of individuals being targeted. Some common segmentation options include:

- Age
- Dwelling type (e.g., rental, detached home, townhouse)
- Education level
- Estimated current home value
- Estimated income
- Gender
- Homeowner status (i.e., rent, own)
- Income
- Length of residence
- Marital status
- National credit rating
- Net worth model
- Person type (e.g., male head of household, female head of household, dependent, retiree)
- Presence of children
- Purchase amount ranges
- Telephone area code
- Year home was built

Response lists are lists of individuals who have purchased something, subscribed to something, or belong to something. These lists are made available by the owners of the list to those interested in promoting things to them. Unlike compiled lists, where the list owners are not concerned about competitive issues, owners of respondent lists will be concerned about what you are promoting to their names and will typically ask to see and approve your promotional materials before allowing permission to use their lists. Additional response selections include:

- Book buyers
- Buyers by ethnicity
- Contest players
- Credit card buyers
- Credit seekers
- Dieters
- Direct mail buyers
- Discount buyers' club members
- Donors (by cause)
- Infomercial buyers
- Internet respondents

Business lists are lists of business people within organizations that can be selected based on geography, type of organization, position or title, and other criteria which may include:

- Annual sales volume
- Business type by Standard Industrial Classification (SIC) or North American Industry Classification System (NAICS) code
- Fortune 500
- Franchises
- High-growth businesses
- Key contacts
- Public or private
- Years in business

There are multiple sources of mailing lists from which you can now order online, where you can determine list counts and costs before making your final selection decisions. A Google search turned up the following first-page results:

- DirectMail.com
- USAData.com
- InfoUSA.com
- AmeriList.com
- UniversalLists.com
- Experian.com

The use of cooperative databases, a recent trend, is having an impact on the list management industry. Cooperative databases bypass the traditional list management and rental market by creating consolidated lists shared by multiple marketers who receive access to the list in exchange for contributing data about their own buyers.

In the nonprofit arena, for instance, the Target Analytics database is used by more than 19,000 nonprofit fundraising organizations around the world. More than 550 of these organizations have submitted their own donor information, which Target Analytics then used to enhance its database of more than 100 million households. Catalogers, publishers, and credit card issuers are also taking advantage of the trend toward the creation of cooperative databases containing the collective contributions of marketers with similar interests.

3. Email List Rules

Online marketers can turn to basically the same list providers they would use when sending direct mail offers through traditional mail. There are some important differences, though, that come into play when using email marketing tactics.

First, the regulations around marketing online are significantly more stringent and restrictive than the regulations that apply to traditional direct mail marketers. While there has always been a tendency for consumers to speak disparagingly of the junk mail that arrives in their mailboxes, the sentiment around the spam that arrives at their desktop is significantly more negative and has led to the implementation of rules online marketers must follow — or risk significant fines.

The American CAN-SPAM Act of 2003 was implemented to protect consumers from unsolicited email promotions. In addition to requiring that marketers send email offers *only* to those who have "opted in" to receive these mailings, the law also requires that marketers provide a fully functioning method for recipients to "opt out" of mailings they receive from online marketers.

Further, the opt-out process must be clear, conspicuous, and easy to use, requiring a *single action*. This means that either the recipient can reply to the email to opt out, or click on a link that takes them to a page where they can opt out of future mailings. Opt-out requests must be immediately honored, and the requester must be removed from any lists that either the marketer is personally using or that it may have shared with others.

CAN-SPAM regulations mean that marketers are significantly at risk if they rent an email distribution list from someone else and send their offer to that list. Why? Because, unless somehow explicitly agreed to, the people on that email distribution list have not opted in to *your* offer. Consequently, the email marketing process generally requires that the list owner conduct the online marketing effort on your behalf. Unlike when you conduct a traditional direct mailing effort and the list owner provides you with a list of names and addresses that you will use, when you do an email marketing effort you will provide the list owner with your email offer and the list owner will send that offer to its list. Further, for any email sent on your behalf by a list owner, the entity that the email is "from" must also have its own advertisement in the email. The "from" sender is the "designated sender" and the entity responsible for processing any opt-out requests. When the "from" sender does not have an advertisement for its own products or services in the email, then any other advertisers in the email (that means you!) become responsible for processing opt-out requests. Of course, since you do not have physical access to the list, you probably do not want to assume responsibility for ensuring that these opt-out requests will be appropriately processed.

Each separate email in violation of the CAN-SPAM Act is subject to penalties of up to $16,000, so noncompliance can be costly. Consequently, when building your own list you will want to make sure that those on your list have specifically opted in to receive email-marketing messages from you. When renting a list you will want to make sure that the list owners —

- send the email on your behalf so it comes from them,

- have built the list based on opt-ins from individuals who have agreed to receive email messages from them, and

- include information on how to unsubscribe from the list as well as an explanation of how they got the individuals' names and email addresses.

The same rules will apply when you are emailing your own list.

In Canada, a similar Act regulates data privacy. The *Personal Information Protection and Electronic Documents Act* (PIPEDA) governs the collection, disclosure, and use of personal information by commercial businesses. If you operate ethically and observe CAN-SPAM rules regarding emails, you are probably (but not necessarily) doing the right thing in Canada too. For more on PIPEDA visit http://laws.justice.gc.ca/eng/P-8.6. Bill C-28, the *Fighting Internet and Wireless Spam Act* was also passed in December, 2010. More information on this anti-spam legislation can be found at www.ic.gc.ca/eic/site/ecic-ceac.nsf/eng/h_gv00567.html.

The bottom line when it comes to email marketing of any kind is that the list you use should be comprised of individuals who have opted in to receive email from you or any list owner you work with, you must be very clear in terms of identifying who you are, and you must make it easy for recipients to opt out of future mailings from you.

Table 2 is a list of email list vendors that appeared in BtoB's *2010 E-mail Marketer Insight Guide* which illustrates the wide range of options as well as the wide range of pricing for email lists.

TABLE 2
Email List Vendors

COMPANY	URL	CPM email lists
Advanstar Marketing Resource Network	http://marketing.advanstar.info	$400 – $475

ALC	www.alc.com	$100 – $325
AllMedia Inc.	www.allmediainc.com	$300
Bethesda List Center	www.bethesda-list.com	$85 – $500
Direct Media Millard	www.dmminfo.com	$200 – $500
Direct Partner Solutions, Inc.	www.directpartnersolutions.com	$150+
Dunhill International List Co., Inc.	www.dunhills.com	$125 – $500
Dunn Data Company	www.dunndata.com	$150 – $400
Harte-Hanks Market Intelligence	www.hartehanksmi.com	$160
IDG List Services	www.idglist.com	$300 – $375
ePostDirect	www.epostdirect.com	$250 – $450
Infogroup/ Interactive-Walter Karl	www.walterkarl.com	$225 – $400
Lake Group Media, Inc.	www.lakegroupmedia.com	$150 – $300
Lewis Direct, Inc.	www.lewis-direct.com	$250
L.I.S.T. Incorporated	www.l-i-s-t.com	$200 – $400
LSC Digital	www.lscdigital.com	$125 – $250
Mardev-DM2	www.mardevdm2.com	$360 – $510
Marketfish	www.marketfish.com	$100 – $850

MCH Strategic Data	www.mailings.com	$200 – $325
MeritDirect	www.meritdirect.com	$225 – $400
MetaResponse Group	www.metaresponse.com	$325
NOBLEVentures	www.nobleventures.com	$90 – $400
PlattForm Advertising	www.plattformad.com	$150 – $450
Postmaster Direct	www.postmasterdirect.com	$100 – $350
Rickard List Marketing	www.rickardlist.com	$250 – $450
Specialists Marketing Services, Inc.	www.specialistsms.com	$150 – $400
Statlistics	www.statlistics.com	$185 – $480
V12 Group	www.v12group.com	$195
Worldata	www.worldata.com	$200 – $500
World Innovators, Inc.	www.worldinnovators.com	$250+

3.1 Co-registration

Because of the idiosyncrasies and risks associated with email marketing, a new technique has emerged to provide access to lists of both consumer and business audiences that may be interested in marketers' offers who have, in essence, "raised their hands" to say, "Yes, I'm interested in hearing about that." This new technique is known as co-registration or Co-Reg.

You've probably seen examples of co-registration if you've subscribed to a magazine offer online or requested a white paper or other free report. You fill out the information required for the subscription you're interested in and then, when your order is confirmed, you're offered the opportunity to receive information about a variety of other products or services. In some cases, you'll be asked for more information after selecting various offers to make sure that you represent a qualified prospect. By doing this you are giving permission for the marketers you expressed interest in to send you email solicitations.

Here's what EdithRoman's website (www.edithroman.com), a long-time player in the direct mail industry, has to say about co-registration:

"The co-registration network is a lead-generation service that captures and sells leads to nontraditional advertisers. Here's how it works: Subscribers to premier top trade business-to-business publications are presented your offer at the same time that they are filling out their individual qualification form. When a subscriber opts-in to learn more about your offer, we deliver you the subscriber's contact information — in real-time — while the sales lead is still hot! This enables you to pay per lead based on data elements you want to collect — from name and email address to full contact information, phone number, and an unlimited array of customizable data elements."

When you're engaged in a co-registration program, you will pay for each of the leads you receive. What you'll pay can vary anywhere from $0.01 to $15.00 (or more) per lead.

4. Finding the Right Lists for Your Business

Choosing the right lists for your direct mail campaign obviously has a major impact on the success of your efforts. A large part of the success will rest on whether you target the right people — those people who are most likely to be interested in what you have to offer. To be the most cost effective, your goal will be to target the fewest to achieve the most. Consequently, the more you know about the people who are most likely to be interested in your offer — and the more clearly and specifically you can define their attributes — the more narrowly you can define your universe of potential purchasers and decrease the number of people to whom you reach out.

While cost is obviously more of a concern with traditional direct mail marketing options because you'll incur printing and postage costs, cost is also an issue with online marketing because you will be paying for the cost of a list in most situations, and email marketing lists are generally more expensive than traditional mailing lists.

Let's take a look at how you might make decisions related to the lists you'll use for your direct marketing efforts. We'll assume that you run a business that sells computer supplies. You've developed a catalog and you want to mail it to some prospects that represent both those on your own list as well as lists you might rent. You'd like to use a combination of both traditional and online tactics.

The first step you might take is to make a list of the types of people who would be most likely to order your products. In this example, your list might include the following:

- Businesses with computers
- People who have computers at home

This is clearly a very broad list. If this was as far as you went in identifying your target market, you could conceivably mail to every business and a large percentage of consumers.

How could you get more specific? You might first start with what you know about the people who have already purchased from you. As you review your database, and because you've done a good job of capturing information about your customers, you're able to determine the following:

- The types of businesses that have purchased from you in the past.
- How large those businesses are.
- Where (geographically) those businesses are located.
- The titles of people in those businesses who have placed orders with you.
- The types of individuals that have purchased from you in the past (e.g., where they live, their annual income, what they use their computers for).

All of these pieces of information suggest possible list segmentation choices that you could make to narrow your field of candidates.

Your next step might be to think creatively about other ways in which the people you'd like to target could be identified. Perhaps through the following:

- Trade associations or groups they might belong to.

- Magazines they might subscribe to.

- Other types of products they might purchase.

Once you know the types of individuals and businesses you wish to target, your next step is researching the availability and cost of lists. List brokers can be helpful here because they're familiar with the list industry and have expertise and experiences that can help you make informed choices. You can also do research on your own online — most of the companies that offer lists provide an opportunity to make list selections online, allowing you to determine both list size and cost.

4.1 Being an informed list renter

Knowing the right things to look for as you search for lists to use in your mailings can mean the difference between a successful mailing and a dismal failure. Following are some important considerations to explore before making a decision to rent a particular list:

- **Source of the names.** Is the list compiled from various sources, comprised of respondents to other direct mail efforts who have made a purchase, or made up of inquirers (people who have asked for additional information, but have not made a purchase)? Be aware as you're reading list descriptions that not all lists, particularly B2B lists, contain names of actual people. Some contain only titles and company names, for instance. This may or may not be what you're looking for. Make sure you know exactly what it is you're ordering.

- **How often the list is updated.** You want the cleanest list you can get with addresses that are current and deliverable — both in the traditional and email environment. Some files are updated only once a year. Of course, no list is going to be 100 percent deliverable, but the more frequently the list is updated, the more likely it is to have a higher degree of deliverability.

- **How old the names are.** When you're renting a list from a business that's been around for several years, it's not inconceivable that many of the names on the list are old — the customers might not have placed a new order for quite some time. You'll want to know what that time period is. Generally, any name that's been inactive for more than a year has questionable value. You may also want to select your list based on recency of purchase (recognizing that you'll likely pay more for more recent purchasers). "Hotline names" may also be available: These are respondents who have replied to a direct mail effort recently.

- **What other offers have been mailed to this list and what offers have been mailed more than once.** This will give you a basis for comparing your offer with other offers that have proven successful. If nobody else selling your type of product or service has used the list with any success, it's unlikely that you're going to break this trend.

- **What selections are available.** While selection options will generally be listed, don't be afraid to ask if you're interested in a selection that you don't see listed.

- **What the minimum order is.** Often, when first using a list, you'll want to test a portion of it. Minimum orders generally range around 3,000 to 5,000 names. Even if the minimum is higher, keep in mind that you don't need to mail the entire list you rent just because you've ordered it.

- **What the addressing and label format alternatives are.** Most lists these days are generated in an electronic format, but you'll want to make sure that the format and fields used will be compatible with your mailing plans, the online software you use to distribute email marketing efforts, or the requirements of your printing or mailing vendor if you're doing a traditional mailing.

- **What data processing options are offered and their cost.** A few options you may be interested in include "merge and purge" (the ability to remove duplicate names that may appear on your own customer files or other lists you're renting), National Change of Address (NCOA) processing to ensure that your traditional lists are as up-to-date as the US Postal Service records, and postal presorts (the ability to sort the mail by carrier route, Zip+4, and/or to bar code your mail). Note that Zip+4 is the traditional five-digit zip code with an added four digits (e.g., 12345-1234) that provide more detailed information to the postal carrier — the five digits would be the city, and the additional digits represent areas of town and street codes.

- **Consider whether or not a sample mailing piece is required.** With most compiled lists a sample piece is not necessary. Owners of respondent lists, however, want to know what kinds of mailings are being sent to their customers so they can guard against what they consider to be objectionable mailings, and so they can keep competitors from mailing competitive promotions at the same time they may be doing a mailing.

- **When to expect the list.** You'll be expected to provide a mail date to the list owner, but you'll want to receive the list early enough that you're able to review it and provide it to your printer or mail house, or email list owner, as necessary.

4.2 Cost considerations

When researching list availability and cost, keep in mind that lower-priced lists are not necessarily your best option. Compiled lists are generally less expensive than response lists; that's because response lists (since they represent consumers or businesses that have purchased similar items) are likely to generate greater results. Similarly, the more specific you get in your list selections, the more you'll pay for the list, but the more narrowly you can define your market, the greater the likelihood of generating results. In general, the higher priced the list, the more narrowly focused it is, and that can represent big benefits.

If you're planning on using traditional direct mail, in addition to the cost of the list you'll also want to factor in the cost of printing and mailing the marketing piece you'll be using. If you're using online direct mail, you won't have these additional costs. In many cases, you'll want to do a combination of both.

Looking back at our computer products catalog example, you will want to consider the various target groups you've identified, and determine which might benefit from a more expensive option such as traditional direct mail. In this case, you may very well decide that mailing a hard copy of your catalog to your past purchasers, as well as contacting them through email, would be worth the extra impact and cost. There may be some response-based list segments that you feel will be highly responsive and so you may want to send them both versions of the mailing as well. In other cases, such as with compiled lists, you may want to initially prospect online through an email marketing effort that offers a hard copy catalog to customers as a way to further qualify the list.

4.3 Placing your order

If you order lists online and receive a confirmation of the elements of your order, that's great. This provides you with the specific details about what you've ordered, which serves as a contract of sorts in the event that what you get is not what you ordered. If you don't have access to this type of confirmation, you'll want to generate your own documentation. This should include:

- **The name of your company.** The list owner wants to know who is responsible for the mailing.

- **Your offer.** Indicate what you're selling and, in most cases, provide a sample mail piece.

- **Your mail date.** Make this date as specific as possible. Most list owners will expect that you adhere to it. If for some reason you can't, you'll likely need to request permission to mail on a different date.

- **Exactly which names you want.** If you don't want to mail outside the country you're in, make sure you request that you be given records only for your country. If you want to make more finite geographic selections, make sure your specifications are clear.

- **The quantity of names you're ordering and the price as you understand it.** This includes added charges for selections and key codes.

- **Your requested delivery date and delivery instructions.**

Once you've received the list, you will want to do a quick review to ensure that it is what you ordered. Check for address format; for example, are all elements of the address present? Are zip codes correct and in proper sequence? Do the names look like the type of prospects you've ordered? For instance, if you've ordered a list of doctor's offices and you see a company name such as "Dave's Pet Suppliers," something is wrong. Do you see any duplicate records? Finally, is the count that you ordered what you received?

Copy and Design

By the time you've begun to consider the development of your direct mail message, and the copy and design that will comprise it, you should have a solid base of information to direct your next steps. You should know what your goals are and you should have a very clear idea of your target audience based on the list selections you've made. Your next step is to translate information about your products and services into key messages that will resonate with your identified target audience.

1. Developing Key Messages

Too often when communicators set out to develop advertising copy, they begin thinking of slogans or headlines. This is understandable, because this is what many of us think of when we think of marketing. It's not the best starting point, though, for developing copy for direct mail communication materials. The best starting point is the development of key messages. Key messages address benefits from the consumer's perspective and differentiate your product or service from your competition.

Key messages can be viewed as bullet points of the *most important* things about your product or service that will allow you to influence the target audience you've identified to pick you. An external frame of reference is critical. The features of your product or service that you are most proud of may not translate into benefits that resonate with your audience … even if those features are very important. In addition, benefits are only meaningful if they are stated in such a way that they position your product or service at a higher level of value than your competitors' products and services.

To illustrate, let's consider the airline industry. Is it a benefit to consumers that the airplane will get them to their destination safely? Yes. Is this a benefit that will serve to differentiate one airline from another? No. Each airline could make this same claim. Consumers *expect* that they will arrive safely at their destination. Therefore, the key message "we are 99.9 percent safe" is not a compelling statement that differentiates you from the competition and, consequently, not the best choice to position your airline against the competition.

This same principle is true for other products and services. Consumers expect a certain threshold level of quality from the products and services they buy. That level varies depending on the industry and the cost of the product. Consumers expect a certain level of performance from the automobiles they buy. They expect that when they eat at a restaurant they will not get food poisoning. These claims — however true — are not effective advertising messages.

Again, looking at the airline industry example, what might be some consumer needs that *would* go beyond standard expectations and might differentiate one airline from another?

- Larger seats
- Better meals
- All first-class … all the time
- Guaranteed on-time service (or your money back)

You can probably think of more. The important point to remember is that your key messages need to focus on those features that *differentiate* your product or service from the competition *and* that are meaningful to your market.

In addition to understanding the needs of your target audience, you will also need to have a good understanding of the product or service you're writing about. A great deal of information probably already exists on your company website, in existing product brochures, and in existing ads. Internal employees are excellent sources of information and should be involved in the process. Spend time interviewing staff to find the answers to some key questions. As you're conducting these interviews, try to think like the customer. Ask questions to help you understand — from the customer's perspective — the key benefits you have to offer. Why should you want to purchase this product? Why should you attend this event? Why should you *act now*?

It's important that you understand your product or service from the customers' or end-users' standpoint. How do they use it? When do they use it? What do they like? What do they not like? What alternatives exist to buying your product or service? What potential objections might consumers have about purchasing your product or service? The answers to these questions will help provide the foundation from which you can develop meaningful, compelling copy that generates results.

Whenever possible, you should experience the product or service yourself. The more information you can obtain, the better you will be able to synthesize this information into the handful of key points that will serve as the basis of your marketing materials. Talk to customers and end users to understand their perspectives. The more you know, the more likely you will be able to identify those specific points that will connect with your audience.

Your final key messages will be nothing more than a bullet list of the most important factors about your product or service ... the kernels of information you will use to develop communication materials which might be used in any of the elements that comprise the media mix.

The AIDA formula is a helpful aid in writing copy for any audience. The AIDA formula, according to the American Marketing Association, "is an approach to understanding how advertising and selling supposedly work. The assumption is that the consumer passes through several steps in the influence process. First, *Attention* must be developed, to be followed by *Interest*, *Desire*, and finally *Action* as called for in the message." This formula is used commonly by copywriters to ensure a focus on results. The following sections discuss how it typically works.

1.1 Attention

Considering the selected medium, how can you capture the attention of your intended audience? Suppose you're using traditional direct mail. What might you do in your direct mail piece to attract attention and "cut through the clutter"?

One important area of focus is the headline. The headline should be used to attract the *right* audience ... the audience most likely to be interested in what you have to sell. If you're selling diet aids, your headline would say something like, "Lose Weight Fast!"

Attention might be generated through the *look* of your direct mail piece, as well. Three-dimensional or unusual formats can stand out and attract attention, virtually crying out to recipients to "notice me"! Developing effective advertising requires a partnership between whoever is writing the copy and whoever is designing the direct mail piece itself.

Generating attention is also important when using email for your direct mail efforts. Here the ability to stand out will be based primarily on the subject line and the *look* of the email. Designing your email in an HTML format allows you to use color and graphic design elements to attract attention. That can be a positive. On the flip side, HTML-formatted emails can look too promotional and result in the unintended consequence of being ignored.

1.2 Interest

To create interest you need to think like your potential customers. When you're writing advertising copy, the focus should be on the customer and his or her needs and not on you, your company, or your product. Instead of telling your audience how your product is made, you want to tell them what your product can do for them.

Before you begin writing, determine what points will most appeal to your target market. Consider the product or service you're marketing, the demographic and psychographic characteristics of your target market, and the medium you intend to use. Then, determine what you want to say and in what order it should be presented. The key to effective copywriting is simplicity and ease of understanding. You don't want to lose your readers by writing something that's confusing or disorganized. Proceed in a logical manner from point A to B to C, etc. A typical structure for a direct mail letter might be:

1. Here's what we have to offer.

2. Here's why we know you'll be interested.

3. Here are the benefits you'll gain by responding now.

4. Here's how you order.

Even when writing for a print medium like direct mail, you will need to think visually and consider how the end user will be receiving and reading your messages. Putting yourself in the position of the reader, consider where that reader will look first. Then where? Then where? Your headline should draw readers to your copy, and then other design elements (e.g., bold-faced subheads, bullet points) should help lead the reader through the copy in some logical manner. Large blocks of dense copy will cause you to lose readers. Subheads that don't represent benefits will cause you to lose readers. Irrelevant or "we"-focused statements will lose readers.

As you write, keep your overall theme or unique selling proposition (USP) in mind. The most effectively written copy is copy that is cohesive; the headline, copy, and illustration all work together and emphasize the same point, which represents a benefit to the readers.

Use the KISS principle: Keep it short and simple. Remember, your prospects don't spend a lot of time focused on any individual marketing appeal. You want to capture their attention and tell them what you need to say as quickly as possible. This means using the most understandable words you can — the shortest words, and the shortest sentences and paragraphs as well. Whether your target audience is teenagers or physicians, you need to convey a simple message. Your audience is busy and your message is competing with literally hundreds of other messages and distractions. Know the points you want to make and make them simply and clearly. Edit your copy mercilessly so that it contains only those "need-to-know" elements that will guide consumers in making a purchase decision.

That said, you should always make your copy as long as it needs to be to allow you to present your key selling points. Ignore anything you've heard about recommended length of copy. There are no hard and fast rules. Your copy simply needs to be as long as necessary to convey your key selling points. That doesn't mean, though, that you should ramble on and on. You should identify three to five key points that directly relate to customer needs and then clearly and concisely provide enough details about your product or service to convince the customer to take action.

Sometimes you can do this effectively with a single line of copy and an effective photo. Consider a full color photo of a tasty slice of pizza, with a single line of copy that simply says: "Hungry?" Sometimes you can't do this effectively without several paragraphs of copy, along with photos or schematics describing your product, how it works, and how it will meet customer needs. Consider a brochure describing a piece of manufacturing equipment that costs several thousand dollars. Always remember that your objective is to convince the consumer to buy. If you can do that in one sentence, do it in one sentence. If not, make your copy as long as you need it to be.

If your key message is not immediately clear, it won't work. You're not going to be in the room with the person who reads your copy, so if you have to explain anything about what you've written, start over or rework the copy until the point you're making is absolutely clear.

1.3 Desire

Desire is created by focusing on and clearly conveying meaningful benefits. The difference between a feature and a benefit is sometimes hard to discern. A simple test to determine the difference is to ask the question: What will the reader get out of the product or service? Your ad should answer the reader's question: "What's in it for me? (WIIFM)" A well-known advertising guideline is, "Sell the sizzle, not the steak." Gillette didn't focus on its razor blade, it focused on the smooth shave.

The copywriter's task is to convert product or service features (from the point of view of your company and its product managers) into benefits (based on the point of view of your target audience). Too often, copy focuses on the features of a product rather than on its benefits. Features are the attributes of a product or service — a statement of fact. For example, "XYZ orange juice has calcium." Benefits answer the all-important question of "What's in it for me?" In this case: "Get the flavor you crave with the vitamins you need when you drink XYZ orange juice." Make sure that your copy goes beyond a description of features to clearly focus on the benefits for consumers. What's in it for *them*?

As you write, you should address any potential reader objections. Consider all of the reasons a prospect might have to *not* buy your product, then write copy to address those objections.

Put your strongest selling point first. You can never know how much of your copy a prospect will read, so it's important to get the strongest information up front. Lead with the key point in the headline and in the first sentence of the first paragraph of your copy. Secondary benefits and selling points can come later.

Body copy makes the sale and should state facts and figures, make benefits clear, convince or persuade, and tell the reader how to respond. Your body copy should derive from the key messages you developed. Copy should be as brief as possible but still tell the entire story, so don't make it unnecessarily brief. If it takes 500 words to explain all the benefits of your services or products and how to purchase them, use 500 words.

When writing copy, keep paragraphs and sentences short, focus on the benefits and not on the features, and be specific. Instead of saying "high quality," translate it into a specific, quantifiable attribute that will be meaningful to the audience. Instead of saying "You'll save money," say, "You'll save $25 each week for the next 10 weeks ... $250 total!"

Think about writing copy as making a sales pitch to a customer. Your goal is to persuade that customer to do something ... most likely purchase your product or service. That involves creating desire.

1.4 Action

You've attracted the attention of your target audience. You've generated interest in what you have to say. You've created desire for your product or service. The next and final step in creating compelling copy is to elicit action.

The purpose of writing copy is to get people to act or react. Beyond this, however, you need to decide whether you want those people to simply remember your company name, whether you want them to visit your website, whether you want them to pick up the phone and "call now to order," or whether you want them to visit their local retailer.

Don't be overly concerned about insulting the intelligence of your audience by being too explicit. It is far worse to assume that the audience knows what you want them to do or how you want them to think of your company and its products or services. Be explicit. If you're creating a response advertisement, *tell* the audience what to do next. Direct marketing advertisers refer to this as the "call to action." Don't leave it to chance that the reader will know what the next steps are. Be specific. "Call 123-4567 *now* to take advantage of this offer" or "Fill out the coupon below for a free lesson." It seems simple and obvious. You'd be surprised, though, at how many advertisers hide their offer within the body copy. Tell your readers what to do, why to do it, how to do it, and ask them to do it.

The offer, as we've already discussed, is the most important part of any promotion, whether you're preparing a brochure, a letter, or an email pitch. What are you selling? Why? What is the price? What's in it for the customer? Your offer should be as direct and straightforward as possible; for example, "Subscribe to this $45 magazine for only $19.95 when you respond by January 1." Don't complicate the offer by trying to sell everything and anything you possibly can. A brochure that attempts to sell a dealership as well as equipment and offers a free catalog will be confusing to the reader and will likely be thrown away before a response decision can be made.

When you're looking for a response, you need to create a sense of urgency. Give prospects a good reason to order *now* while they're thinking of your product and have your advertisement in their hands. Such language as "limited quantities available," "limited time to order," or "special price only in effect until such and such a date" can do the trick.

Even when you're writing nonresponse copy (perhaps an informational brochure about your company), your copy should still be action-oriented. How do you want the audience to feel about your company? What do you want them to do with the information you're providing? An instruction as simple as "visit our website for more information on … " can help to generate action on the part of your target audience.

Throughout the process of writing copy, keep in mind that an effective communication effort is not necessarily what you like. It's not a campaign that wins awards (unless winning awards was your objective). Effective communication achieves results.

Consider that the same is true of *any* communication efforts. If you're involved in employee communications how do you measure effectiveness? Hopefully based on quantifiable results that meet clearly defined objectives. Sharing information is not enough. Achieving results through the sharing of that information — whether you're writing an article for the employee newsletter (with the intention of raising awareness of some organizational effort or changing perceptions about a contentious issue) or a direct mail postcard to generate orders for your product — should be the goal of any communication effort.

2. Tips for Writing Great Copy

The following key points will help you create action-oriented copy.

2.1 Compose a benefit-oriented headline

In order to effectively catch the attention of your target market, you need to offer a clear benefit as quickly as possible. The headline is the best place to do this. Your headline serves two primary purposes: it catches the attention of the reader and it selects your audience.

You want your headline to present an immediate benefit to those people who are most likely to buy your product. For example, if you're selling a weight loss program, your headline might read: "Lose 15 Pounds in 10 Days." There is an immediate benefit and the audience has been clearly defined; obviously those people who do not need to lose weight will not be interested. Those who are interested, however, will be drawn in by the obvious benefit and will read on. In writing benefits — whether they appear in a headline, body copy, or the PS — always remember to focus on the target audience and not on yourself.

2.2 Write with design in mind

Even if your copy will be presented in a letter and won't involve any actual design, design considerations should come into play as you compose your copy. You want the piece you're creating to be visually appealing and to invite readership. You can do this by using short sentences and paragraphs, indented paragraphs, bold and underlined phrases, bullet points, marginal notes, and plenty of white space. Make your copy easy to look at and it will be easy to read.

2.3 Read it out loud

Remember your copy is your sales pitch. Whether you're writing a radio script which will be verbalized or newspaper copy, you need to consider how it sounds. The best way to do this is to read your copy out loud. You'll be surprised at the little glitches you'll notice when you do this. It's a simple technique to tighten and improve your copy.

Also, don't be the only judge of your copy. Show your copy to other people, preferably people who don't know exactly what you're trying to do. Do they understand? Are all points clear?

2.4 When to include PS

When using a letter format, always include a postscript (PS). The PS is the most read part of a letter, second only to the headline. Take advantage of this opportunity to reinforce a selling point or repeat your call to action.

2.5 Simplify your wording

If you can simplify the words you've used, do it. The average reader reads at a seventh-grade level. Even if your audience is comprised of PhDs, you should still try to adhere to the KISS principle at all times. If you use $50 words, you'll lose some readers, alienate others, and call more attention to your word choice than to the message you're trying to convey.

2.6 Learn from the competition

You can learn a lot about your product and potential market by analyzing your competition. First, recognize who your competition is. Then, analyze how they've positioned their product. Who are their target customers? What are their selling propositions? What are their pricing strategies? What do you feel they're doing right? What do you feel they're doing wrong? How can you improve on their strategies?

2.7 Back up any claims you make

Consumers today are more savvy than ever and they won't believe unsubstantiated claims made by advertisers. If you say your product will do something, provide evidence that this is indeed the case. This evidence could be scientific studies, case examples, or testimonials. The more evidence you can provide, the better you'll be able to make a strong sales argument.

2.8 Use testimonials

Quotes, stories, and examples from satisfied customers can help to reinforce your selling claims and substantiate the benefits you present. Whenever you receive an unsolicited testimonial, immediately ask for permission to use it in your advertising materials — with the individual's name. Solicit testimonials by encouraging customers to contact you with comments, questions, etc. Keep a file of these materials so you can easily access them when you're preparing your next piece. Always use a name with the testimonial. If possible, include a company name and city as well. You might also include a photograph along with this information.

The more you can do to make the testimonial giver "real" to your prospective customers, the more impact the testimonial will have.

2.9 Make a reference to your website

Refer prospects to your website for additional information. The Internet provides great benefits to marketing communicators. When torn about bogging down an ad with too much information so you can appeal to those hard-to-convince readers, you now have the ability to direct people to your website where you can offer a wealth of information to meet the needs of your most skeptical prospects.

2.10 Know when it's time to hire an expert

Copywriting is an art. Good copywriters can drive sales of your product or service upward. Poor copy that doesn't motivate consumers to buy is simply a waste of your money. A newspaper ad that doesn't persuade is a bad investment. If your ads aren't getting the results you'd like, it may be time to find outside help. It can be worth every penny!

2.11 Quick tips for better results

The following quick tips will give you better results:

- When listing items, have an odd number finish the list, such as 3, 5, or 7. Just as when arranging pictures on a wall, asymmetry attracts the eye.

- When using direct mail, a first-class stamp will out-pull metered or bulk mail. The letter is more likely to get opened when it has the appearance of legitimate — not junk — mail.

- Certain colors are more effective than others. Red suggests action and immediacy. Yellow can have the same effect. Blue and green are calm colors that are effective in a company brochure in which you want to establish an image of professionalism or stability, but not so effective when you're looking for action or response.

- When pricing your products, don't round the numbers. Studies show that customers respond better to a price like $19.98, for instance, than they do to $20.

- If you use a picture, include a caption. A picture may be worth 1,000 words, but it helps to add 10 to 20 words of your own. Tie the caption to your key messages.

- Never use sans serif type (the kind of font without the "feet," such as Arial) for body copy. It's more difficult to read. The serifs (with "feet," such as Times New Roman) help pull the eye naturally through the copy.

- Be careful about asking questions in your headline. If the customer can answer the question with "No," he or she is not likely to keep reading.

- Include plenty of dingbat-type symbols in your copy. Dingbats are the little symbols such as arrows, bullets, check marks, and starbursts that help break up your copy and can be used to highlight important sales points.

- Don't use all uppercase letters in a headline. It may give a bold impression, but it's too difficult to read.

- Pay close attention to your order form design, whether print or online. The order form often fails to remind the prospect of why he or she should order, so remember to restate the offer clearly, provide precise instructions on how to order, and ask for all the necessary information. (For more information about order forms, see Chapter 6.)

3. Writing for the Web

While much is the same about writing direct mail copy for online distribution as it is for the traditional realm of direct mail, there are a few key differences. First, web writing is briefer, more succinct, and designed to be more scannable than traditional direct mail copy. Online readers are more impatient than those reading traditional messages, so you want the key points of your copy to stand out clearly and immediately.

Second, writing for online distribution allows you to use links which can serve as a means of leading readers to more detailed content if they're interested ... and because of online analytics, you can tell whether or not they are! The use of links can allow you to find a good balance between trying to tell it all and trying to whet the appetites of your target audience so they're willing to click through for more.

Third, writing in the online world requires at least a basic understanding of SEO, or search engine optimization. Since your ultimate goal with any online content is to drive traffic to your website (sometimes through a landing page), ensuring that any copy you write contains the search terms and phrases that those interested in what you have to offer are likely to search for can help you boost your search ratings.

Finally, writing for online distribution requires consideration of words and phrases *not* to use because they are likely to be targeted as spam by Internet service providers (ISPs).

While SEO and spam avoidance may make many direct mailers' eyes glaze over, the concepts are not that difficult to understand and manage to ensure the best results from your online activities.

3.1 Search engine optimization (SEO)

When customers and potential customers identify a need for whatever it is you have to offer, how might they search for that need online? In other words, what specific words or phrases might they enter in the search field on Google to try to find products or services like yours? Those are the words or phrases that you should make an effort to include in the copy you write. Including those terms in your copy makes it searchable simply because those words and phrases are there. It's that simple. The better you are at identifying the possible words and phrases that might be used and the more often you use them in everything you do, the more you increase the odds that your website will rise higher in the rankings, simply meaning that you'll show up sooner on the list of results that searchers receive when they enter the word or phrase.

You're not likely to win in the search wars by using very general terms. For instance, if you sell women's clothing, the phrase "women's clothing" is just too broad and likely to be used by too many online marketers to allow you to ever stand out. That's where the *long tail search* comes in, and it's a technique that can be especially useful for small businesses.

Frank Dale is vice president of Compendium Blogware (www.compendium.com). Dale focuses on the long tail search in his work with clients. Long tail searches are simply those that are based on longer search phrases; for example, "size 11 red men's Nike running shoes + California" versus "running shoes." Long tail search holds promise for site owners attempting to compete with large content providers. Importantly, search engines are finding that users are using longer, more specific search phrases to find detailed answers. By targeting the specific terms most related to your business's products or services, you can compete for the most valuable customers.

Smaller businesses can, and do, win with long tail search phrases — win meaning that their websites show up higher in the list of results returned by the search engine.

Alhan Keser is CMO for Blue Fountain Media, a web design, development, and marketing company in New York. Another key point about long tail search, Keser notes, is that they have a higher conversion rate (the percentage of visitors who actually make a purchase). "The reason for this is that someone looking up a product or service using very specific words is most probably at a more advanced stage of the buying cycle than someone searching for a generic term," Keser says.

Although it can seem a bit overwhelming, much free information is available on SEO tactics (Google offers some of this).

3.2 Spam

Internet service providers (ISPs) use various algorithms to identify which emails are legitimate and which may represent spam, or unwanted email to their customers. When these algorithms come across certain words or phrases, they may "kick out" the email so that it never arrives at the end user's mailbox (where it might also be relegated to the junk mail file). That's not a good thing. The *worst* thing that could happen is that your company is identified as sending so many emails considered to be spam that you are banned from distributing email by certain providers. That's not likely to happen to most users, but those who attempt to blatantly undermine the system and send unsolicited messages to massive numbers of recipients with little to no interest in what they have to say will find that they run afoul of the ISPs as well as CAN-SPAM or PIPEDA or other laws.

What can cause your emails to be kicked out? ISPs make decisions based on a number of things, ranging from spam complaints received from users about emails they've received from you to the identification of the use of certain words or phrases that scream spam or might otherwise raise red flags about the appropriateness of the content (e.g., pornographic messages). If you look in your own junk mail file, you may find messages from various disreputable marketers that contain incorrect spellings or a combination of letters, numbers, and symbols to represent certain words. These are basically attempts to trick the spam filters into allowing the email to get through.

The best way to avoid running afoul of these filters is to adhere rigorously to CAN-SPAM and other requirements and ensure that any messages you send are sent to recipients who have opted into your list, or who have opted into the third-party lists that you may be using (sent by the third party on your behalf). Another red flag is sending email messages too frequently. That can mark you as a spammer. Besides being marked as a spammer, you should also be concerned about the number of messages you send to any audience. Email fatigue is real and you don't want to overdo it.

Beyond this, and from a copywriting standpoint, it's perhaps even more important in the online world to make sure that your copy and messages are directly relevant to the recipient and to avoid over-the-top hyperbole that can be immediately marked as spam. Of course, arguably, these practices are equally valuable in the traditional direct mail realm.

The words you use in your subject line are particularly at risk for identifying your message as spam. There are certain trigger words that can mark your email as spam even though you may be following all the rules and communicating with a very narrow list of recipients who are eager to receive your message! SendBlaster Blog lists 200 spam words and phrases to avoid on its site.[1] Here are a few of them:

- Free (e.g., free hosting, free investment, free leads, free membership)
- Great offer
- Guarantee
- Gift certificate
- Call now
- Act now
- Risk free

Basically, these are the types of words and phrases generally associated with advertising pitches.

It can also be interesting and a bit overwhelming to take a look at the list of rules included in the algorithms used by SpamAssassin, a popular open-source spam filter.[2]

Rather than trying to avoid the trigger words and warning signs that will cause your email messages to be marked as spam and captured by the spam filters, which can certainly defeat even the most

---

[1] "200+ Spam Words and Phrases to Avoid in Your Email Newsletters," http://blog.sendblaster.com/2009/10/19/200-spam-words-and-phrases-to-avoid-in-your-email-newsletters, accessed March 18, 2011.

[2] SpamAssassin, http://spamassassin.apache.org/tests_3_3_x.html, accessed March 18, 2011.

enthusiastic copywriter's creativity, you can take advantage of free online tools to check the content of your email promotions. Lyris ContentChecker for Email is a free, easy-to-use spam-filter utility that helps you identify potential content issues and improve your email messages before you hit the send button. Lyris uses the SpamAssassin content filter to validate email-marketing campaigns against the multiple rules that are used by various receiving domains and assigns a spam score to your content. While having a low score doesn't guarantee that your email will reach the intended recipient's inbox, having a high score will *certainly* count against you.

The Federal Trade Commission (FTC) offers the following tips for avoiding CAN-SPAM violations (which can result in penalties of up to $16,000 per email) and, consequently, for improving the odds that your emails will reach their marks[3]:

- **Don't use false or misleading header information.** Your "From," "To," "Reply-To," and routing information — including the originating domain name and email address — must be accurate and identify the person or business who initiated the message.

- **Don't use deceptive subject lines.** The subject line must accurately reflect the content of the message.

- **Identify the message as an ad.** The law gives you a lot of leeway in how to do this, but you must disclose clearly and conspicuously that your message is an advertisement.

- **Tell recipients where you're located.** Your message must include your valid, physical postal address. This can be your current street address, a post office box you've registered with the US Postal Service, or a private mailbox you've registered with a commercial mail receiving agency established under the Postal Service regulations.

- **Tell recipients how to opt out of receiving future emails from you.** Your message must include a clear and conspicuous explanation of how the recipient can opt out of getting email from you in the future. Craft the notice in a way that's easy for an ordinary person to recognize, read, and understand. Creative use of font size, color, and location can improve

---

[3] The *CAN-SPAM Act: A Compliance Guide for Business*, http://business.ftc.gov/documents/bus61-can-spam-act-compliance-guide-for-business, accessed March 18, 2011.

clarity. Give a return email address or another easy Internet-based way to allow people to communicate their choice to you. You may create a menu to allow recipients to opt out of certain types of messages, but you must include the option to stop all commercial messages from you. Make sure your spam filter doesn't block these opt-out requests.

- **Honor opt-out requests promptly.** Any opt-out mechanism you offer must be able to process opt-out requests for at least 30 days after you send your message. You must honor a recipient's opt-out request within ten business days. You can't charge a fee, require the recipient to give you any personally identifying information beyond an email address, or make the recipient take any step other than sending a reply email or visiting a single page on an Internet website as a condition for honoring an opt-out request. Once people have told you they don't want to receive more messages from you, you can't sell or transfer their email addresses, even in the form of a mailing list. The only exception is that you may transfer the addresses to a company you've hired to help you comply with the CAN-SPAM Act.

- **Monitor what others are doing on your behalf.** The law makes clear that even if you hire another company to handle your email marketing, you can't contract away your legal responsibility to comply with the law. Both the company whose product is promoted in the message and the company that actually sends the message may be held legally responsible.

4. Templates and Tools

Few small-business people also have skills as copywriters or designers, but fortunately there are tools, templates, and options available to you. For copywriting, there are many freelancers and agencies that provide these services (more about this in section **5.**). For basic design, today's word processing programs offer the ability to do simple formatting and design to incorporate different fonts, type sizes, use of color, etc. There are also templates and tools available that can help immensely:

- Microsoft Office offers online access to templates for creating flyers, brochures, and other types of layouts (http://office.microsoft.com/en-us/templates/CT010104303.aspx). Best of all, they're offered at no cost (of course you need to be using Microsoft products to take advantage of them!).

- Templates are also available through HP (Hewlett-Packard) (www.hp.com/sbso/productivity/office/brochure.html).

- Other online fee-based services are also available and can be found by simply doing a search for "brochure templates."

For online communications, templates are readily available through the various service providers that offer distribution services such as Constant Contact, RatePoint, iContact, VerticalResponse, and others. There are multiple options available, and most programs allow you to make your own changes to layout and color and are fairly easy to use.

While templates can be a great benefit to small businesses, one drawback when using pre-designed layouts is that many others may also be using the same layout or design. As your company grows you may be more concerned about your brand and overall image, so this may become an issue for you. In many cases, however, these templates will serve you well.

5. Using Outside Resources

Many small businesses and entrepreneurs can't afford to hire full-time writers or social media experts to aid in their direct mail efforts. Fortunately, there are many opportunities to get assistance on a part-time or freelance basis.

The first step in selecting a partner — whether an agency or individual — is knowing what you're looking for. Identify your objectives. What do you want to accomplish? Are you looking for one-time development of image materials (i.e., logo, letterhead, Yellow Pages template), or are you looking for the development of a campaign and an ongoing relationship? Do you have specific sales targets you want to reach?

What you want is integrally tied to what you can afford to spend. Establish your budget before developing your list of potential agencies. Depending on the industry you're in, you may be able to obtain information from trade associations about the average advertising and marketing budget (as a percentage of revenue) for your industry. Ask business contacts if they would be willing to share with you how they establish their budgets. Or, develop your budget based on a percentage of the anticipated sales volume you expect the campaign to generate.

You should provide each firm or individual you're considering with the budget you have to spend. It's a critical part of the evaluation process. Suppose you have $200,000 to spend. Some agencies may say, "We can't even begin to develop a campaign based on that size of budget." You will be able to eliminate them from consideration. Those agencies still in the running can provide proposals to you that will fit into your budgetary framework. You want a good indication of what they will be able to do for you based on the resources you have available.

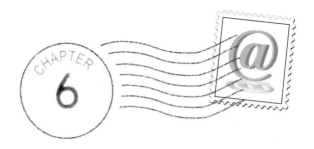

Creating the Order Form

The order form is often the most overlooked aspect of the postal direct mail piece, which is unfortunate because it's arguably the most important. The order form often fails to —

- remind the prospect of why he or she should order,

- restate the offer clearly,

- provide precise instructions on how to order (you'd be amazed at how many people forget to include a return address), and

- ask for all the necessary information.

An important best practice when designing the order form is to involve the people who process orders when they're received. They will be able to help you lay out a form that includes all the information they will need to most efficiently process the order. However, be sure that you don't go overboard in attempting to make things easier for your staff at the expense of your customers. The easier you can make it for your customers to place an order with you, the more likely they are to do so.

1. Make Your Order Form Logical and Orderly

An order form should be visually open and attractive and it should look like an order form. Cute designs may cause confusion and may get overlooked or be unused. For example, an order form shaped like your product (let's suppose your product is a digital camera) is cumbersome and difficult to use. Order forms are best kept traditional (i.e., rectangular or square) and, if at all possible, located on the bottom edge of the mailing piece where they can be easily removed.

Number the steps on your order form to help people easily see what they need to do. Make it as clear and simple as possible. It can be costly to your company to process orders when the customer hasn't provided all the necessary information or hasn't included all the necessary charges. You can use color or shading to highlight important elements of the order form.

Whenever possible, try to limit the number of options on the order form. A cramped order form discourages sales and slows down the purchase process while the prospect decides which option he or she prefers.

If, however, you're offering a number of different products, make sure that you list them all and include space for the customers to indicate their selections. Requiring customers to fill in a lot of information that you could just as easily have provided will not enhance your chances of receiving a positive response. If you simply have too many product selections to include them all (e.g., a catalog) and you must require customers to fill in information, include a one-line example to clearly indicate how information should be completed.

2. Give the Customers All the Information They Need

First, be sure to restate your offer on the order form as clearly and simply as possible. Begin your order form with wording that indicates a positive decision on the part of the respondent such as:

- Yes, I would like to order ...

- Please send me ...

- Please rush me ...

Your order form should read as though the customer is writing to you.

If you're offering a choice of terms, make sure that each choice is clearly indicated and separated and that it's clear to the respondent how to indicate his or her selections.

You should include an anticipated delivery time. The US Federal Trade Commission (FTC) mail-order rules, often referred to as the "30-day rule" by marketers, require that you state a delivery time in your promotion and that you must have a "reasonable basis" for expecting to ship within that time. If no time is indicated, you must ship within 30 days of receiving a properly completed order. If you are unable to meet these delivery dates (e.g., due to out-of-stock merchandise), you are required to give the customers that information, along with an option to cancel their order.[1]

Put your shipping charges on the order form and explain them clearly. There are a number of different approaches to collecting shipping and handling. The most common include the following:

- **Based on weight and distance.** You must provide weight information for each product in addition to a chart which the customer can use to determine distance charges.

- **Based on an item-by-item charge.** A specific shipping charge is indicated for each item.

- **Flat fee.** You simply state, "add $X for shipping and handling."

- **Per item charge.** "Add $2.00 shipping and handling for each item ordered."

- **Based on order value.** "When ordering $5 to $50, add $X for shipping and handling; $51 to $200, add $X."

Don't forget to list sales tax. Sales tax must be collected in any state where you are considered to have a nexus or presence; in Canada the rules are by province. This presence could take the form of a warehouse, a salesperson, or a high degree of activity.

Be sure you include the name of your company and your address on the order form as well as on each individual part of the promotion. Even if you're providing a return envelope, your name and address should be on every piece of the mailing. These individual pieces can be easily separated and you can't know which portion your respondent will hang on to.

You should always provide clear instructions for the return of products as well. You want to avoid the problem of products being returned without adequate identification of the purchaser.

3. Offer Multiple Order Options

While including a traditional order form is still important to make it as convenient and immediate as possible for customers to act, today's technology makes it possible for customers to order in various

---

[1] "Mail and Telephone Order Merchandise Rule," http://business.ftc.gov/documents/bus02-business-guide-mail-and-telephone-order-merchandise-rule, accessed March 18, 2011.

ways in addition to filling out and mailing a traditional order form. They can, for instance, call a toll-free number from their landline or mobile phone, or they can visit your website to place an order online, and many will do this. Make sure all of the ordering options are prominent on your order form so customers can select the option that will work best for them.

4. Additional Order Form Tips

Here are some additional tips for designing effective order forms for your direct mail efforts:

- Place the order form in a prominent spot — make it easy to find, whether in a catalog, in a brochure, or on a website. Don't make customers have to look hard to figure out how to order from you.

- Make sure that your order form looks logical and orderly. Keep it visually open and attractive and make sure that it looks like an order form.

- Avoid legal-sounding terms or very formal order forms.

- List your highest priced items first.

- Consider the use of a nontransferable order form to add a sense of exclusivity to the offer. A nontransferable order form would be for use only by the recipient and could not be used by someone else.

- Even when offering a call-to-order option, encourage customers to fill in the order form before calling — this will save time for your phone operators and keep your lines open and accessible to others.

- Add impulse items to the order form.

- Ask for a street address for UPS delivery.

- Date your prices and your mailers to indicate when offers expire and how long prices are valid.

- Use color or highlighting to draw attention to important elements of the order form.

- Restate your offer on the order form as clearly and simply as possible. Begin your order form with wording that indicates a positive decision on the part of the respondent, such as, "Yes! I would like to order … "

- If you're using a written form, ask customers to print the information requested. Make it difficult to not print clearly by providing boxes that only accommodate one letter or number per box. This will make it easier for data-entry people to decipher names, addresses, etc.

- Clearly state the prices and terms of your offer.

- Ask customers to provide both daytime and evening phone numbers, indicating that they may be used if there is a question about the order. A side benefit: You're collecting phone numbers which can be added to your customer files for possible telemarketing applications.

- Ask for an email address as another convenient method of staying in contact with your customers.

- Request "ship to" as well as "bill to" information, especially if you sell items that are frequently purchased as gifts. This not only allows you to accurately process orders and bill the appropriate person, but gives you the opportunity to build a prospect file as well as a customer file.

- When using traditional mail, remember to code your order form on the form itself or on the mailing label, so you can capture the tracking information you'll need to analyze response. Consider the use of peel-off mailing labels. You'll get your coding information back and you'll also have legible name and address information for your order-entry personnel to read.

- Don't forget to thank the customers for the order!

5. Online Ordering

All of the fundamentals of order form design apply as equally to online ordering as they do to ordering through the mail. However, online ordering represents both additional challenges and additional opportunities. The challenges relate to moving the consumer through the ordering process as efficiently as possible. The opportunities relate to the ability to very specifically track online activities.

The ability to code order forms to identify different lists, different offers, different messaging, etc., has always been a big benefit for direct mailers as they continually evaluate the effectiveness of their direct mail efforts through quantifiable information that can help them improve virtually every aspect of the promotion. Even *more* information is available when using digital direct mail.

5.1 Analyzing traffic patterns

An example of a very successful online retailer will help to illustrate this. Valerie Holstein started e-tailer CableOrganizer.com with her husband in her garage with a $30 investment. Seven years later, the company earned more than $13 million and, despite the recession shows no signs of slowing. Originally focused on tools to organize cord clutter, the company's product line has expanded to include electrical supplies, network products, home theater components, tools, and testers.

Holstein calls herself "the queen of SEO (search engine optimization)," stressing that she takes a very analytical and thorough approach to analyzing website activity and listening, *really* listening, to customer feedback. This enables the company to be both responsive and innovative. She and her staff continue to pay close attention to the feedback they get through web analytics and customer and site visitor feedback. The information helps trigger improvements in the site and identifies new products that customers are interested in.

"We track the ranking of incoming links for targeted key words," says Holstein. "We track how many links we get from blogs, from forums, and sites like Facebook or Twitter, and we look at the traffic that is generated from these people linking to us. We also look at customer feedback — and we get a lot of it." Content on the site is designed to be "keyword rich." That leads to indexing by Google, which increases traffic to the site. "It's a great, great resource for people and all of this brings our ranking up," she says. "When people find what they want it means they're coming back — it increases traffic and unique visitors and you have a domino effect."

If it sounds simple, it's really not. "We use the Kaizen theory of constant improvement," says Holstein. "We run millions of tests on the website every day." Literally. "We do our testing very seriously and as scientifically as possible," she says. Some of the things tested and modified on the site include text colors, color combinations, placement of words, word choices, vocabulary, button shapes — yes, even button shapes! In addition to testing based on web tracking, Holstein employs usability testing to provide insight into how people actually navigate through the site and engage with it. "We hire people to come in for a half-hour and put them in front of the site and say 'Okay, find this product.' We have a camera that tracks their eye contact so we see when they make comments if what they say matches their eye contact." Why is that important? Because sometimes people try to be "nice," she says. "They'll try to be nice and say 'This is fine,' but they're looking someplace else."

All of the listening, researching, and testing is critical, Holstein says. "When you work for seven years on the same website, you lose perspective. It's absolutely crucial to have a new set of eyes."

5.2 Abandoned shopping carts

While most businesses won't go through this level of detailed analysis, at a minimum they should evaluate the process that users go through once they've responded to an online mail promotion. The easier it is to order online, the more likely it is that orders will be placed.

Shockingly, even after your prospects get to your order form, they may change their minds. The result is abandoned shopping carts. This is the term for the online phenomenon in which customers put merchandise into their virtual online shopping cart but then fail to complete the sales process.

You've probably seen it from time to time in the brick-and-mortar world as well — shopping carts containing merchandise that have been abandoned by shoppers for reasons unknown. It seems, though, that this phenomenon is much more prevalent in cyberspace.

In fact, according to Forrester Research,[2] 88 percent of web buyers say that they have abandoned an online shopping cart without completing a transaction. Think about your own online purchasing behaviors and you'll probably be able to come up with at least one instance in which you did the same. The research further — and perhaps surprisingly — indicates that these numbers have not changed over the past five years, meaning there is still ample opportunity for online retailers to make changes in the ordering process to address the reasons for abandonment. Obviously, even incremental changes can add up to big dollars if fewer orders are abandoned. What are some of the most common reasons for abandonment? According to Forrester, they are:

[2] "Understanding Shopping Cart Abandonment," www.forrester.com/rb/Research/ understanding_shopping_cart_abandonment/q/id/56827/t/2, accessed March 18, 2011.

- Shipping and handling costs were too high (44 percent)
- I was not ready to purchase the product (41 percent)
- I wanted to compare prices on other sites (27 percent)
- Product price was higher than I was willing to pay (25 percent)
- Just wanted to save products in my cart for later consideration (24 percent)

Monitoring your abandonment rates over time and exploring opportunities to decrease those rates can be very important to your direct mail efforts. Of course, the checkout process is only part of the answer. Even before consumers get to this point, some other issues apply — first, cost. Consumers obviously want to know what they're paying for and how much they will pay. Making pricing and shipping information clear and specific can help avoid later surprises that cause consumers to change their minds.

The beauty of online direct mail marketing, though, is that even when people do abandon the purchase process you can often identify them and attempt to bring them back into the fold through what has become widely known as "remarketing."

5.3 Remarketing

Remarketing has become a buzzword in online marketing circles. It simply refers to reaching out to those who have proceeded into the online purchasing process or "sales funnel" only to abandon their shopping carts at the moment of truth. According to a 2009 survey by Advertising.com and SEMCO, remarketing has been shown to improve ad response by up to 400 percent across several Advertise.com clients, compared to traditional display marketing.

Remarketing is the high-tech version of "second mailings" in the traditional direct mail world, but with the added benefit of knowing *exactly* where in the purchase cycle the consumer was stopped from placing the order. Using their database management systems, traditional direct mail marketers can track who did or didn't respond to a direct mail effort, but they can't tell whether the consumer ever actually saw the piece, looked at it, whether the person began to fill out the order form, or if he or she picked up the phone to call the customer service line.

Through online analytics, marketers can tell, and they can reach out specifically to people who had gotten close to the purchase point, but backed out for some reason. Even something as simple as asking for an email address very early on in the order process can provide you with information that you can use to reach back out to a highly qualified prospect. Another very commonly used technique is asking people to register on the site before placing an order. That way you can easily tell if a registered user started and then gave up on an order. Your shopping cart technology also likely has a recovery system in place to allow you to see users and recontact them.

Subtlety is important, of course. Consumers are understandably concerned about online privacy and how their personal information is being used, so you want to avoid tactics that may be overtly "big brotherish." Large e-tailers such as Amazon.com use remarketing techniques regularly and are so good at them that you may not even know that you've been remarketed to!

Hiring Help

While many of the activities involved in direct mail marketing — whether traditional or online — can be do-it-yourself, there may come a time when you feel that you could benefit from the use of outside help. This can be particularly true when looking for creative services (e.g., copywriting or graphic design) or technical assistance with Internet-based marketing activities such as search engine optimization (SEO) or online advertising. Fortunately, there are a wide range of options available today, from traditional sources (e.g., running a classified ad in the local paper) to online freelance service providers like Elance (www.Elance.com). This chapter will give you some tips and recommendations on how to find the help you need and how to evaluate the various options available to you.

1. Where to Find Advertising Help

Referrals can be the best source of information when you are trying to find qualified agencies or freelancers to work with you on your advertising. Ask colleagues or business contacts about the experiences they've had with various vendors and who they would recommend. This can provide you with a list of "first contact" vendors to start your search. Beyond referrals, there are a number of sources for advertising or marketing agencies:

- Internet
- Yellow Pages
- Competitors
- Companies whose advertising you've admired

- Colleagues

- Associations

- Trade publications (e.g., *Advertising Age*)

Another good source of information is your local media representatives. They work with agencies regularly and may be willing to tell you which agencies have good reputations both in terms of creative ability and administration (i.e., submitting materials and paying bills on time, etc.).

Turn to colleagues in your community or various trade or professional groups you've been involved in. Have they used freelancers? Could they refer you to someone? Local associations may also be a good source of information.

When looking for graphic design or technical writing assistance, local printers can often provide you with leads. Printers work with these types of people regularly on projects, know their work, and are usually glad to provide you with information on who to contact.

Ads in the local paper are still an option, particularly when you're attempting to recruit from your community. Just as when you're looking for full-time help, local classified ads can be a good way to build a file of résumés or interested people that you can refer to when jobs arise. In addition to local advertising, online services such as Craigslist now allow you the ability to advertise for assistance literally around the world. The proliferation of these sites have led to an abundance of individuals and organizations offering a variety of communication-related services at very reasonable rates.

Networking is the key. Be alert to the many sources of information around you and build a file of possible contacts, including what services they provide, how much they charge, who they've worked with in the past, and how you learned of their availability.

2. Working with Interns

Universities, technical colleges, and even high schools can be good sources of energetic, enthusiastic, and low-cost or no-cost assistance. An internship is an educational experience that provides students with the opportunity to work in a real-world setting and apply what they have learned in the classroom while evaluating whether the experience supports their interest in a particular field or profession. Internships allow students to translate theory into practice and can be an excellent way to reinforce material learned in a classroom setting. Internships are most effective, though, when interns are actually able to apply the skills that will help them eventually pursue their desired profession.

The first question you're likely to have when considering the use of interns is, "Where do we find them?" Local schools are a good starting point to explore intern opportunities and availability, but before making that contact you need to answer some key questions.

First, will the internship be paid or unpaid? Organizations can pay interns in addition to having students earn academic credit, or have the internships be unpaid, in which the students solely earn academic credit. Not surprisingly, paid internships are the most desired by students. Another consideration for employers is whether they can legally offer unpaid internships. The decision of whether or not to pay interns in the US may be impacted by the US Fair Labor Standards Act, which regulates unpaid internships, and the Department of Labor, which enforces the statute. Nonprofit organizations are allowed to have volunteers; however, for-profit employers must meet a six-part test to determine if an internship can be unpaid.[1] The criteria include:

- The internship, even though it includes actual operation of the facilities of the employer, is similar to training which would be given in an educational environment.

- The internship experience is for the benefit of the intern.

- The intern does not displace regular employees, but works under close supervision of existing staff.

- The employer that provides the training derives no immediate advantage from the activities of the intern, and on occasion its operations may actually be impeded.

- The intern is not necessarily entitled to a job at the conclusion of the internship.

- The employer and the intern understand that the intern is not entitled to wages for the time spent in the internship.

The next question is, "What will you have the intern do?" Before contacting a school, clearly define the role or project and have a good idea of the type of individual who would best fill that role. The process is really not much different from hiring an employee for any

---

[1] "Fact Sheet 71: Internship Programs Under The Fair Labor Standards Act," www.dol.gov/whd/regs/compliance/whdfs71.pdf, accessed March 18, 2011.

position ... the goal is to match the individual with the requirements of the position to achieve a win-win situation for both parties. Having clear objectives, a solid structure, and a willingness to commit time and energy to the relationship will have a significant impact on the success or failure of your interns.

3. Working with Independent Contractors

Looking for temporary assistance is much the same as looking for full-time help. Before you make any calls, determine what your needs are. If you're looking for graphic design help, what level of experience will you need? Help in developing a simple order form will require different skills than help in designing and preparing a full-color annual report that you'd like to distribute in both hard copy and online formats.

There are two primary ways of evaluating the skills of freelancers: portfolios and references. When you contact a freelancer and arrange a meeting (whether in person, via phone, or even via video or web conferencing), ask the candidate to bring along samples of work that have been done in the past. As you review the work, pay close attention to the style, the amount of detail required to complete the project, and how well the work parallels your own needs.

An important question to ask when reviewing this material is "How much of this work did you do on your own, and how much was in collaboration with company representatives or other outside assistance?"

References are another important way of determining the qualifications of freelancers you interview. Ask for names of people the freelancer has worked with and permission to contact those references. Then be sure to make the calls. When you contact references, you'll want to ask the following:

- What types of projects did you assign this individual?
- Were you pleased with the final work product?
- Were deadlines met?
- Did you run into any problems along the way and, if so, how were they resolved?
- How much direction was required?
- Would you work with this individual again?

Another caution for businesses using freelancers and contractors is to make sure that they are truly contractors and not employees and therefore subject to tax withholding requirements in both the US and Canada. In the US, according to the Internal Revenue Service (IRS), the general rule is that somebody can be classified as an independent contractor "if you, the person for whom the services are performed, have the right to control or direct only the result of the work and not the means and methods of accomplishing the result."

There are also a number of common-law rules that can help to determine whether someone is an employee or an independent contractor. These fall into three categories: behavioral control, financial control, and the type of relationship between the parties. This includes:

- Whether the individual is given direct control about where and how to work (e.g., hours of work, types of tools or equipment to use, an order or sequence to follow, specific individuals to work with).

- The level of training provided. Employees generally receive training; independent contractors use their own methods.

- The extent to which the worker has unreimbursed business expenses.

- The extent to which the worker is able to make himself or herself available to others.

- Whether or not the business provides the worker with employee-type benefits such as insurance, vacation pay, sick pay, etc.

In Canada, the criteria are very similar and generally involve four areas: control, ownership of tools, chance of profit or risk of loss, and the level of integration between the contractor and the client which refers to the contractor's ability to work with other clients.

The fines for not correctly classifying individuals as employees can be significant, so it's important to make sure that those you consider to be contractors really are contractors and are not subject to withholding laws. Government websites in the US and Canada provide detailed information to help make these determinations:

- In the US: www.irs.gov/businesses/small/article/ 0,,id=99921,00.html

- In Canada, guidelines vary by region, but the Alberta page includes links (at the bottom) to other regions: www.canadabusiness.ab.ca/index.php/operations/335-contractor-or-employee-guidelines-for-alberta

4. Working with Agencies

Just as when you're selecting an intern, contractor, or employee, you should outline specifically the traits, characteristics, and skills that are required to meet your unique needs when working with an agency.

Use the criteria you've developed to prescreen the list of potential partners you've assembled. Once your list is narrowed down, select two or three candidates to interview on a formal basis. When doing your final evaluation use a formalized evaluation form, comparing each candidate against the same criteria in much the same way you would evaluate candidates for employment within your company. This process helps you maintain objectivity in the evaluation process and helps to ensure that you don't overlook a key factor. Some factors to consider:

- **Industry experience.** Select a partner that has experience working with businesses in your industry. You'll benefit from the knowledge they've gained working with other industry players and learning from their successes and failures.

- **Size.** Do you want to be a big fish in a small pond or a small fish in a big pond? There are advantages to working with a large agency such as experience, reputation, broad range of expertise, and resources. However, there are also drawbacks. With a smaller budget you may not get as much attention as the agency's larger clients. You may be working with junior staff members who are "cutting their teeth" on your account.

- **Cost.** The size of the agency is often directly related to the cost of the agency's services. On the one hand, larger agencies have higher overheads and consequently may be priced out of your ability to pay. On the other hand, these higher costs are also associated with access to a broad variety of high-level skills and resources.

- **Capabilities.** Ask each prospect you evaluate to provide you with work samples (keeping in mind that simply "looking good" is not enough; results are what matter). If possible, visit each agency to see firsthand the facilities, staff, and resources the agency has to offer. In addition, you'll want to ask each agency to provide you with information about their capabilities. You want to know what they can do for you. You will want the agencies to give you specific information on how they will handle your account, including creative, media, and production services provided. Also find out how may clients they've served and why they're particularly qualified to assist you.

- **References.** Ask each agency to provide you with a list of current and former clients. Contact each client and ask for additional referrals. Find out if these clients have been satisfied with the work produced for them. Do they feel the work done for them was a good value and investment? Did they experience any problems? Would they select this partner again?

- **Right fit.** You have to like the people you will be working with. When evaluating agencies, it's important to know whether the people you're meeting with are the people who will actually be assigned to your account. If not, ask to meet these people. Consider how well the people you will be working with understand your industry and your company. Do they ask good questions? Do they listen carefully to your responses? Are they comfortable disagreeing with you based on their expertise and experience? You do not want an agency that simply does what you say. You are not an advertising expert; if you were, you wouldn't need to work with an agency!

5. Finding Help Online

The Internet now offers many opportunities to find talent around the country — or even around the world — to help with multiple aspects of your direct mail activities, from writing copy and creating design, to designing websites or landing pages, evaluating results, etc.

Craigslist is one of the most widely known sources. It can be thought of as an online "help wanted" site. It's easy to use and it's basically free! Some areas do charge for job posts such as in the San Francisco Bay Area and New York; however, there is no cost to respond to these listings.

Elance is another popular site frequented by those in the marketing and media relations industries, among others. For a one-time fee of $10, you can set up an account and begin posting jobs immediately. Those interested will apply for and bid on the job and you select the person who best meets your needs. You may also choose to use the site's featured listings, for which you pay $15 per posting. The upside is that Elance can be a great source of very inexpensive talent. The downside is that the quality of candidates ranges across a broad spectrum and many users are not English-speaking, so when looking for help with writing copy for English-based prospects or customers, this can be an issue.

Crowdsourcing has become another popular option used by businesses to find support for their projects. Crowdsourcing, a relatively new term (said to have first been used by Jeff Howe in a June 2006 *Wired* magazine article) refers to the practice of outsourcing tasks that might previously have been assigned to a specific freelancer or contractor to a large group of people through an open call. What makes crowdsourcing so powerful is the broad response from a wide range of individuals which requires no cost. Those who present their ideas, projects, or solutions are paid only if their ideas are used.

For instance, 99Designs is a website that provides crowdsourcing for graphic design projects. Services that can be crowdsourced range from logos to website design to T-shirt design to banner ads, etc. You can host a design contest where a crowd of designers compete. Tell them what you need, how much you'd like to pay ... the more you offer, the more design concepts you'll see. Then tell everybody what you like and don't like. You check out all the designs until you get the match you're looking for; if you don't like any, you can get your money back.

6. Communicating with Freelancers and Agencies

Advertising and marketing agencies and freelancers can provide a real boost to your marketing communication efforts by providing you with the expertise and assistance you need to more professionally and successfully promote your products and services. Be sure to evaluate and select your partners carefully. There are literally thousands of agencies to choose from. Not all will be right for you.

Once you've selected a partner, whether an agency or individual, managing that relationship effectively is critical. Establishing clear objectives and expectations and clarifying roles can help to avoid problems and misunderstandings.

There are certain challenges inherent when working with people who are not regular, full-time employees. Their time is not solely committed to you and you may be competing with other clients. You do not have direct control over freelancers' output, so you may not see how the work is proceeding until it's completed. Clear, direct, and effective communication is the key to making this relationship work.

One key point is to respect the expertise of the partner you've selected and resist the urge to become directly involved in the creative process. Recognize that your role as the client is to provide the agency or freelancer with your objectives; information about your company and its philosophies, culture, and desired image; information about the products and services you wish to market; and general, overall direction. It is *not* your role to write or rewrite copy, to develop headlines or themes, or interfere in any other way with the process. Just as when you write copy internally and help manage the process through a focus on key messages, when you're serving in the client role your review should be based on adherence to agreed-upon objectives and messages. Don't wordsmith. Don't attempt to serve as creative director. To work most effectively with communication partners:

- Share information freely. Provide your agency or freelancer with background information about your products and services, past communication efforts and results, and market research information.

- Provide clear direction. Know what you want and be clear about expectations.

- Be accessible. Be responsive to calls and emails.

- Focus feedback on key messages and objectives.

- Establish and communicate expectations and report back on results.

- Hold your partners accountable for agreed-upon results.

6.1 Before you begin a project

Gather the materials that the person will need to do the job. If you're having somebody help you write a brochure, pull together the appropriate background material that will be needed. Be thorough. Have prices, product descriptions, telephone numbers, website information, etc., prepared and available for the freelancer so that everything can be provided up front. The more background information you can provide or direct the freelancer to, the less time he or she will need to spend gathering his or her own background information and the more you'll save.

6.2 Know what you want

If you don't have a clear idea of what you want at the outset, or aren't able to communicate it to the freelancer, you're bound to be disappointed with the finished product. That's how costs can creep up as you go through revision after revision after revision.

Unless you really want to say, "Just do what you feel is best," and are prepared to live with the results, be able to clearly indicate the kind and quality of work you expect. Be specific, too, about what you expect the freelancer to do. If you're working with a designer, will you want that designer to be responsible for obtaining printing bids? If you're working with a writer on a newsletter, will the writer be required to gather the information and conduct interviews, or will you supply the background material?

6.3 Have a budget in mind

Think about what you expect to spend, not only for the freelancer's time, but also for any printing or production of the materials being created. If you only have $500 to spend, you will not be able to print and mail 10,000 copies of a full-color brochure and pay the freelancer's fees.

6.4 Put it in writing

Don't trust yourself to remember the details of your agreement. To avoid confusion, misunderstanding, and frustration later, put the terms of your agreement in writing. This includes details of what you will provide, what the freelancer will provide, what the deadlines are, how much you will pay, and what you will pay for.

6.5 Keep in touch

Once you've assigned a project, don't just forget about it. Establish agreed-upon meeting times to check on the progress of the project as it's being developed. This may be nothing more than a phone call to see how things are going, or it may be a meeting to discuss the project in more detail. Remember, freelancers are employees too. They deserve the same considerations you give to your staff members. When working with freelancers:

- Don't assume too much control. You're hiring this person for his or her expertise so let him or her handle the project.

- Don't be too critical. If you don't like something, say so and explain why. Focus on the big picture and don't waste your time and the freelancer's time worrying about small details such as word choice, type selection, colors, etc. That's the freelancer's job. That's what you're paying for.

- Do provide plenty of direction in terms of the results you're looking for. The clearer you can be about the requirements of the job, the better chance you have of receiving a completed project you'll like.

- Do give positive feedback first. For example, "This is what I like about your layout … " If necessary, you can follow up with, "I'm concerned, though, about … "

- Do realize that it can take time to find the right fit. You may work with a number of people before you find one that can quickly understand what you want, deliver a finished product on time, and consistently turn out quality work.

Format Options and Opportunities

Three key elements in embarking on a direct mail campaign include:

- A product to sell.

- A list of potential buyers.

- Compelling key messages to cause your target audience to act.

There is another key element which is the direct mail *package*. There are a variety of different format options that you might choose to deliver your traditional or online direct mail message. The choices you make should be based on your objectives and audience, as well as a consideration of what others are doing and how you might "break through the clutter" to achieve maximum impact. As we'll also discuss, you may choose to use these various options in combination to increase the odds that your message will be received.

1. Traditional Direct Mail Packages

The classic direct mail package, in the traditional direct mail environment, has historically consisted of a letter, a brochure, and a response card or business reply card (BRC) inserted into a #10 envelope. In some cases, marketers have also included what is known as a "lift note" — a small note generally printed on a slip that is folded and contains a headline or teaser. The name originated from the idea that this additional note would provide a lift in response.

Interestingly, even though most merchants rely on orders via phone or over their websites, BRCs are still common. They provide a visible and direct way of asking for the order. Tip: If you're asking for credit card or other personal information (as opposed to using a two-step sales approach in which you're just asking the respondent to express interest in learning more), include a business reply envelope (BRE) so that this personal information will be protected.

Today, with the advent of the Internet and as more and more direct marketers compete for the same marketing dollars and for the attention of consumers amid growing piles of junk mail, mailing formats have expanded beyond this traditional package to include a variety of hard copy and online formats using increasingly more creative techniques to capture attention.

Of course, the reason direct mailers turn to these unique formats is to increase the odds that their sales messages will stand out from the myriad of other messages bombarding their potential customers each day. If your message gets noticed, the theory goes, it will get opened and read.

Another important function of these packages is getting past the notorious gatekeepers — particularly in the B2B environment. The gatekeepers, either the staff in the mail room that sort and deliver the mail or the assistants who may screen the mail for their bosses, have a critical role to play in determining what gets delivered and what gets relegated to the trash can. Here, direct marketers have been known to create packages that look like official government mail, packages that look like important express mail delivery, packages that contain plastic "charge cards," packages that make use of striking holograms, and a variety of other unique ploys to capture attention and ultimately generate an order.

In the virtual world, the "junk mail" or "trash" folder is a significant gatekeeper with online marketers increasingly challenged to ensure that their email marketing messages actually reach their mark. Similar techniques are used to capture the attention of the recipient. In both traditional and online environments, though, marketers need to be cautious to not cross the line between capturing attention and irritating — or even infuriating — their intended recipients. Consumers don't like to feel tricked and using deceptive methods to capture their attention can often backfire.

2. Letter Mailings

While the direct mail package is an industry standard, a simple letter mailing (a letter in a #10 envelope) can be an effective and inexpensive means of getting your message to your intended audience, and is often used in the B2B market. But direct mail letters are different from general business correspondence. There's an art to writing direct mail letters that generate results and it includes some techniques that you wouldn't typically see in a traditional business — or personal — letter (not that many people write personal letters anymore). Marketers can benefit from zigging when the competition is zagging. Using direct mail letters (the traditional snail-mail kind) can get results.

The most important aspect of the direct mail letter is the copy. While you can hire freelancers or work with an agency to help develop your copy (discussed in Chapter 7), there's no reason that you can't also try your hand at writing a sales letter designed to generate results. The following sections include some tips to help you write your sales letter (note that these same methods will also serve you well when creating email marketing messages).

2.1 Identify your audience

No matter what type of promotion you're using, identification of the target audience is a crucial first step. Ask yourself the following questions:

- Will you be mailing to your own customers? If so, which customers and what makes them unique?

- Have the customers all purchased a similar product in the past?

- Has each member of the target group made a purchase within the past six months?

- Have they all spent a minimum dollar amount?

- Are they all relatively new customers?

- Are you targeting new potential customers?

- On what basis did you make your list selection?

- What do you know about this audience?

- What interests do they share?

When you have identified your audience you can move on to defining your offer.

2.2 Define your offer

Offers are key in direct mail because what you are trying to do is generate a response. Unlike image advertising where you're simply attempting to make people aware of your product or service and generate interest, direct mail is designed to elicit an action of some sort. That action is driven by your offer. So, once you've chosen a group of people to market to, you need to identify your offer as precisely and clearly as possible. Before you can begin to write the direct mail letter you need to know what it is you want your readers to do. Be specific.

Importantly, don't complicate the offer by trying to sell everything and anything you possibly could. If you have a cleaning services franchise, a letter that attempts to sell a franchise as well as equipment and offers a free catalog will be confusing to the reader and will likely be thrown away before a response decision can be made. Focus is the key.

2.3 Outline your letter

Once you've determined the market and composed your offer, the next step is to outline the letter. Proceed from point A to points B, C, D, etc., in a logical manner and you're less likely to lose your audience. A typical organizational structure for a simple direct mail letter might be:

1. Here's what we have to offer.

2. Here's why we know you'll be interested.

3. Here are the benefits you'll gain by responding now.

4. Here's how you order

5. PS: Here's what we have to offer.

As you can see, successful direct mail letters work in a circular manner. If the offer you've outlined in the headline and repeated in the body copy is somehow overlooked, you want your prospects to pick up that same bit of information in the PS — the most-read part of any letter.

2.4 Compose a benefit-oriented headline

In order to effectively catch the attention of your target market, you need to offer a clear benefit as quickly as possible. The headline is the best place to do this. A benefit is a direct value for your audience.

When you write a benefit headline, you don't want to make your audience work to infer the benefit. For instance, a headline such as, "XYZ Company Introduces Its New Product Catalog" would require your prospects to stop and think. What they'd be thinking is, "So what?" and chances are, you'd lose them immediately. A better headline that would focus on the audience might be, "New Cleaning Products at Prices Competitors Can't Beat — Guaranteed!" This would be more specific and directly suggests target audience benefits.

2.5 Get to the point

Put your offer up front. When writing ad copy of any kind, it's important to keep the prospect reading. You want to lead that prospect through the letter — you don't want attention to lag. Assuming your headline attracted attention, your prospect is now at the introduction of your body copy. To maintain your prospect's attention, you need to immediately pick up on the benefit offered in the headline and expand that benefit to focus on the offer.

2.6 Convey a clear selling message

A good direct mail letter will do four things:

1. Introduce a benefit.

2. Reinforce the benefit (as many times as necessary).

3. Ask for the order.

4. Close.

Any extraneous information introduced in the letter will cloud your offer, create confusion, and probably result in your letter being tossed into the nearest recycling bin.

2.7 Write with design in mind

Even though one of the benefits of using direct mail letters over brochures is that you don't need to hire a graphic designer, design considerations *do* come into play as you compose your letter. Your letter can be visually appealing if you use several reader-assisting techniques such as the following:

- Short sentences

- Short paragraphs

- Indented paragraphs

- Bold and underlined phrases

- Bullet points (like these)

You can even get fancy within the text of your letter by using an additional color, penciling in margin notes to draw attention to certain phrases, circling parts of the letter, etc. Put yourself in the reader's position as you review your completed letter. Would *you* be likely to read this correspondence if it crossed your desk or landed in your mailbox at home? If not, you need to make some changes.

2.8 Personalization

One of the benefits of using letters to generate sales is the ability to personalize your sales message. Today's printing technology allows a wide range of personalization options, from the use of the recipient's name (first, last, or both) to the insertion of other pertinent and specific information, such as prior purchase history or other relevant data that you have in your database.

Other ways to personalize your mailings include adding a handwritten note, hand-signing the letters, writing in margin notes, etc. These techniques are only practical for small mailings. With larger mailings, use technology to help you approximate the look of a personal message.

3. Catalogs and Brochures

Catalogs and brochures remain the stalwarts of the direct mail industry, although today's catalogs have decreased dramatically in size compared to the massive Sears catalog of years gone by. Catalogs generally incorporate full color and, because of their expense, are usually sent to customers whose purchase histories suggest an ongoing interest or in some cases, lists of highly targeted response files from similar retailers.

Brochures come in a variety of shapes and sizes. The format you choose will be based on a combination of the desire to capture attention (which may result in a choice of format that is different than what others are using) and the need to both follow postal requirements and manage costs (more about this in Chapter 9). Format options include decisions about both size and folds or finishing options. The format you select will also be driven by the information you have to present — the more information, the larger the size requirements. Because of the ability to use traditional direct mail to drive recipients to websites for more information, smaller formats are becoming increasingly common. In fact, postcard mailings have become a very common, inexpensive, and effective choice for traditional mailings.

4. Postcards

When we think of postcards, we may tend to think of the typical, travel-sized versions that we send back home when on a trip. While that size is used, it's more common to see larger-format postcards designed to stand out in the mail and get the attention of recipients through the use of strong and colorful graphics and visual elements. Postcards can be a variety of sizes (again, depending on postal requirements), and are basically flat pieces with copy on both sides. They have become such a popular format that there are companies such as PostcardMania that make the use of postcards their primary offering to clients.

PostcardMania offers three sizes of postcards:

- Standard: 4.25″ x 6″

- Jumbo: 6″ x 8.5″

- Colossal: 6″ x 11″

Postcards are often used as part of a two-step marketing process, generally designed to capture the attention of the recipients and drive them online for more information.

5. Product Samples

Sending product samples through the mail is an old practice that is still used and effective. Who doesn't like to get something free in the mail? Mailing product samples is done primarily to introduce consumers to a product they may not have heard of or tried in the hopes that they will start buying. What a great way to use the mail to literally get your product into the hands of your potential customers!

In the B2B environment, the specialty products industry often mails product samples (e.g., pens) to business prospects. The product serves both as a sample and as a dimensional element designed to capture attention.

6. Dimensional Mailings

Dimensional mailings can take a variety of formats ranging from the very simple (a letter envelope with a pen inside) to a fold-out brochure that opens into a pop-up replica of a product, building, or other graphic image. You are limited only by postal regulations and budget. The expense of these formats, both in terms of printing and mailing costs, can be worthwhile, but primarily for high-cost items. In the B2B environment, dimensional mailings are commonly used as a method of getting past gatekeepers. A package is more likely to convey importance than a brochure or letter mailing. Dimensional mailings also often have more staying power as recipients tend to keep these mailings, particularly if they're unique.

7. DVD and CD Mailings

Back in Chapter 1 we talked about some interesting results from a 2010 study that offered compelling evidence for the use of DVD and CD mailings. Even though consumers could technically access the same information online through a link sent via email, something about receiving the hard copy in the mail generated better results! While this can be an effective form of direct mail marketing, as with dimensional packages, the decision to use them will be impacted by higher cost and greater complexity. For higher priced products and services, though, this is an option that should not be overlooked.

8. Email Marketing

Email marketing — from simple pitches in text-based format, to HTML-formatted full color and graphics appeals, to longer form e-letters — has emerged over the last several years as a strong contender and competitor for traditional direct mail efforts. There are several reasons for this, but the most obvious are —

- the rapidly increasing number of people online, with email accounts, and

- low cost since email marketing involves no print or postage costs.

While most email marketing efforts are quite blatant, a modified approach makes use of e-letters. E-letters, or newsletters that are distributed via email, can be a great way to stay in touch with an existing audience, reach out to new prospects, and raise awareness of your products and services on an ongoing basis. Commonly used by professional services firms (e.g., consultants, attorneys), e-letters are a more subtle form of direct mail marketing, as their implied purpose is to inform. Beneath the information lie subtle, and sometimes not-so-subtle, offers to engage with the professional services firm or purchase anything from subscription services to webinars or other training programs.

There are a number of low-cost options available for the creation and distribution of e-letters and other email marketing efforts. Some of the most popular companies are Constant Contact, RatePoint, VerticalResponse, and iContact. Each of them offer various pricing options based on the size of your email list, how often you wish to send email marketing messages, your use of images, archives, and reporting capabilities. The key considerations in selecting a package are quality of design, flexibility and ease of use, and cost. Most packages will offer you a variety of templates from which you can choose, eliminating or reducing the need to have design skills (or to hire someone who does). However, options vary and can be somewhat limited in terms of how easy it is to make changes to these templates, so that's something you will want to consider.

9. Choosing a Format

All of these techniques offer opportunities to make an impact. From the unique to the traditional, your decision of which format to use will be based on goals or objectives, audience, and budget. Traditional and basic formats don't have to mean ineffective. A simple letter mailing can be as effective as a three-dimensional package with a DVD or CD inside! As we've discussed, other driving factors include your choice of list and how effectively you're able to quickly and compellingly convey your offer and key benefits to your market.

Suppose you're selling a line of clothing designed for pregnant women. The product (i.e., clothing) demands four-color treatment. It's difficult to portray clothing in black and white in a way that will convince customers to order. Photography, design, and layout will be important as you promote this type of product.

Your budget may dictate that you can't afford a 64-page, full-color catalog. So, you may decide to develop an initial campaign that consists of a postcard that will drive people to your website where they can view your product offerings.

If you have a self-published book called *How to Be a Great Manager*, your product would not need to be conveyed in full color or even require a traditional direct mail approach. An online, e-marketing effort may be all you need.

When selling high-ticket items you may find that high-cost promotions (e.g., dimensional mailings and the use of DVDs and CDs) make sense for you. You'll also want to ensure that your promotional materials adequately represent the quality of your product. It would not make sense to send a 4.25″ x 6″ black and white postcard to promote a timeshare vacation in France.

Today's decisions about format have both benefited from and become more complex because of the advent of online options. It is unusual today to find examples of when just one approach, in isolation, is used effectively to generate sales. A direct mail campaign often incorporates multiple elements and options to drive sales.

10. Combining Options in a Direct Mail Campaign

As with any type of marketing, it is often a combination of efforts that best generates results and not any one individual effort. In the old days it was common for direct mailers to do a follow-up mailing, which they referred to as a "second mailing," to generate additional inquiries or orders. Sometimes a third or fourth mailing would also be done. Technology has made it possible to eliminate those who have already responded from these follow-up mailings (assuming the order hasn't been lost in the mail or in cyberspace), so that prospects aren't frustrated by receiving more than one offer.

Today, direct mailers can take advantage of both traditional and online options in combination to boost their success rates. As one marketer shares: "One of my regular clients has used direct mail for years to promote his training courses; I have been writing his sales letters since 2004. In the early days we sent the mailed letter only to his extremely targeted list of customers and prospects. Over the years this campaign strategy has developed and now we send a pre-mailing advance notice by email to existing and previous customers who have said they are happy to receive emails. We then send the letter by post — using live stamps. We then follow up with a sequence of email reminders." This combination of efforts, she says, serves to reinforce and remind the audience and leads to good results.

The challenge, of course, lies in planning, scheduling, coordinating, implementing, and evaluating the effectiveness — individual and summative — of these efforts. The time is worth the effort, say those who have benefited from using a combination of traditional and online methods (including social media — see Chapter 11) for their direct mail efforts.

10.1 Leveraging traditional direct mail and online options

Josh Mabus, principle of Mabus, an advertising agency, in Tupelo, Mississippi, is one person who still believes in the power of traditional direct mail marketing. Much has changed in the direct mail industry over the past 20 years, says Mabus. But, a lot has also stayed the same. What has stayed the same are the basic principles of identifying and connecting with target markets to encourage them to take some desired action. What has changed is the ability for even very small businesses to inexpensively and effectively target small market segments with personalized messages in very creative ways. The printing industry, the postal industry, and the advent of the World Wide Web have all had significant impacts on the direct mail industry.

Personalization and the ability to integrate campaign elements across different media are two of the key benefits that Mabus takes advantage of as he works with clients to target very specific, personalized messages to very specific audiences. Much of Mabus' work is with universities that are targeting their messages to high school students who are beginning to consider options for their college careers.

The use of variable data printing allows these colleges to send brochures that are personalized not only based on the names of the recipients, which can appear in various places on the piece, but also in terms of the images that are on the piece that can be targeted based on gender and ethnicity. In fact, there are so many opportunities for the inclusion of unique, variable data that when Mabus shows potential clients an example of a piece that includes only the generic information, it's basically blank, he says. Better yet, the cost of creating these highly targeted pieces has declined significantly because of the technology that makes such printing possible. In the old days it would have been unheard of and very expensive to do a run of 50 full-color brochures. Today, variable digital printing options make it cost effective to do just that.

"I can create a high-quality direct mail piece for 50 people for about $3 to $4 a piece," says Mabus. Better yet, that piece is highly targeted and uniquely created to resonate with each individual based on their personal characteristics and preferences.

Technology makes it possible to combine hard copy and online promotions in personalized ways, notes Mabus. Through the use of personalized URLs (or PURLs), recipients of mail pieces can be directed to web pages designed just for them. A student who receives a brochure from a particular college, for instance, might be directed to visit johnsmith.suchandsuchcollege.com — a unique page designed only for John. The site would reflect the same look and feel as the mailing piece. Once there, the prospective student might be asked to fill out a brief survey about his or her academic and personal interests. Based on these responses, another even more highly targeted and interest-specific response piece could be sent to the student focusing on those elements of campus offerings that match his or her identified interests.

Email promotional efforts can also be part of the mix and can be timed to coincide perfectly with the delivery of a hard-copy mail piece to the student's mailbox through the use of intelligent mail bar codes, which work with USPS mail in the same manner that FedEx and UPS packages are tracked. "We know in real time when a direct mail piece will go in a mailbox," says Mabus. "This is such a tremendous advantage over anything we've had before." The more marketers are able to coordinate the delivery and receipt of multiple messages about the same offer, Mabus notes, the more impact their message will have. You don't know when a prospect will drive by your billboard, or read your ad in a magazine, or even see a commercial on television. But today's technology allows direct mailers to know exactly when their mail piece is delivered to a mailbox, when their email message is delivered and opened, and when the prospect visits his or her personalized web page or clicks through to a link for a landing page. "There's a multiplicative effect when I can send you a piece of mail and an email at the same time," says Mabus.

Some might ask whether in these days of Twitter and Facebook, direct mail is really an effective way to reach high school students. Mabus asserts that it absolutely is, for a couple of key reasons:

- In the same way that many adults may be desensitized to receiving direct mail offers in their mailboxes, kids are desensitized to the messages they see on sites such as Facebook, often not even attending to the messages that come their way — especially when those messages are promotional rather than social, says Mabus.

- In addition, Mabus notes, getting something in the mail is a "special event" for those in high school. They don't get much mail. "That physical, hard, tangible piece of mail carries weight to it that nothing else we've found does," he says.

Direct mail in its traditional form is not going away anytime soon, asserts Mabus. "In my opinion snail mail is very much alive and will exist as long as people exist. Human beings are tactile organisms. It's the only way we have to deliver something that I can touch and feel and that's tangible."

Direct mail in its traditional form will continue to be augmented by new innovations that can help to extend its reach. Mabus sees the traditional direct mail piece as the hub of a number of other, related activities that the original piece might generate. "I see a dotted line going from the direct mail piece to a website, to an email, to a cell phone," he says. "Anything I can do to extend the life, the effect, and the impact of that piece by integrating it with your life will help me accomplish my goals."

Kodak offers a good case example of how direct mail can be combined with online media to achieve significant results. Kodak's 2006 "Play Ball" campaign offered recipients a chance to win a trip to the pro-baseball championship in exchange for registering at a landing page that collected survey information from respondents. The campaign is a good example of how traditional direct mail can be combined with online options to generate interest, gather additional information about prospects, and build relationships. The campaign used direct mail, web, and telemarketing. Approximately 10,500 prospects were targeted through purchased and in-house lists representing three B2B segments:

- Commercial printers with 20-plus employees or more than $5 million revenue

- In-plant printers with 10-plus employees

- Digital service bureaus — prepress service bureaus, digital printers, direct mail advertising services

The direct mail piece used a Major League Baseball (MLB) theme and offered a dream package giveaway for two to the first game of the 2006 World Series. Six mail drops were executed from May to August, 2006. Variable printing was used to depict 28 variable cover images featuring the major league baseball stadium closest to the prospect's address.

Respondents were directed to a web page that built on the direct mail piece in terms of look and feel. The landing page registered prospects for the offer and collected survey information to drive additional variable messaging for the fulfilment package.

The fulfilment package, which was sent as a follow-up to those who visited the landing page, included a full color MLB stadium poster and a baseball card with a photo of the digital print solution sales manager based on the prospect's location and including their "stats" (i.e., contact information). Also included was a small-format thank you/confirmation letter from the regional sales manager.

The five specific techniques that Kodak used to help get its messages across to its target audience were highlighted in *Deliver* — a publication from the USPS. The techniques were:

1. Variable design promoting the campaign's baseball theme by incorporating one of 28 great stadium images with the Kodak brand elements and logo. Respondents received an image of the baseball stadium closest to their geographic location.

2. The mailer included the value proposition for the Kodak NexPress Solutions and Kodak DirectPress Solutions for a specific vertical market, such as education or health care, based on the recipient's area of interest.

3. Copy focused on a topic based on the vertical market. For the education market, for example, the lead emphasized that educational institutions face competition in recruitment as well as budget pressures that require any print solution to come with a solid return on investment (ROI). The content focused on opening the door to data-driven communication using digital solutions from Kodak.

4. The mailer spotlighted two solutions, but also identified other services from Kodak, including business evaluation, business development, and training services.

5. Woven through the narrative was the concept of Kodak as the best partner to help grow your business. The partnership concept is the lead on the website landing page and continues

in the messaging of a follow-up reminder email for those who did not immediately respond.

The campaign achieved $5.02 million in revenue, with more than 500 future interest leads generated. Options for multi-platform campaigns are many and continuing to expand. Another emerging option that holds potential for direct mailers is quick-response codes.

10.2 Quick-response codes

Quick-response (QR) codes represent the most recent innovation and serve to extend the reach of direct mail and other printed materials to the mobile environment. QR codes are matrix barcodes that can be read by mobile phones equipped with cameras or smart phones. Similar to a barcode you would see on a product in a retail environment, QR codes are arranged in a square pattern on a white background; the codes can contain text, URLs, or other data. They are truly revolutionary!

QR codes were created in Japan by Denso-Wave, a Toyota subsidiary, back in 1994. The codes allow anyone with a mobile phone to scan the QR code and decode its content. The content (most typically a URL) generally takes the user to a specific website. The use of these codes basically removes the need for people to have a pencil and paper handy to write down information. They simply scan the QR code and the information is captured in their mobile device. For instance, it could be used to put information on a calendar — you walk by a poster for a play, scan the QR code, and voila! The info is captured and stored in your phone. Or, you receive a direct mail piece in your mailbox for a new restaurant in town that contains a QR code — you scan the code and are taken to the website where you can see menu items and prices.

QR codes can be printed on any hard-copy format, from business cards to newspapers and magazines, to signs, products, etc. Users can generate and print their own codes by visiting a variety of online sites where the codes can be generated for no charge (e.g., http://zxing.appspot.com/generator).

11. Printing Considerations

Since we've seen that not only is traditional direct mail still a viable option for many marketers but is also a potentially important part of an integrated campaign, there's a good chance that you will need to consider printing options when planning your direct mail efforts.

When you need to have material printed, you're faced with a variety of options: from standard materials available from specialty vendors to the local quick-print shop, to larger, commercial printers and even online resources that can help drive down costs. How do you determine which is right for you?

While you could also print off materials on your office printer using templates available from various office supply stores (and there's certainly nothing wrong with this if the quantities you're looking at are relatively small), when you're dealing with more complex projects or larger quantities, it's usually more economical to go to a commercial printer.

The best advice about using printers is to become familiar with the options in your area. Visit or call the printers in your area. Most printers have sales representatives who will be more than happy to come meet with you. Their experience with a myriad of other clients means that they often have much advice and insights to share about what has worked for others and may also work for you.

When you meet with a printer, ask to see samples of the work they've done in the past. Find out what they specialize in, what type of equipment they have, and what clients they've served. Then call those clients and find out whether they were happy with the service and product they received. From these efforts, you should be able to select three or four printers who you feel will be able to do the work.

Today, you also have the option of working with online printers and there are literally thousands of them! As when selecting any vendor, it's important to do your research, check references, and proceed carefully. Test a few smaller projects first.

Bidding is the most common way to get information from printers on pricing. Since each job is different, it's virtually impossible to simply get a standard list of charges. You will need to approach printers with a specific job in mind and compare one printer's costs against another. This is known as bidding.

Many printers can help you with this process by providing a form known as a "spec sheet" or "bidding form." This form allows you to describe the job in terminology the printer can understand and use to determine the cost of the job. Today, many printers offer convenient online access to these forms and bids can be quickly and easily attained.

The printer will want to know the size of the piece you'll be printing, how many ink colors you will want to use, what type of paper stock you will print on, and whether you will be using photographs and, if so, how many.

Get bids from multiple printers — both local and online — to give you a range of pricing options. While price should not be the only consideration in your selection, it will certainly be a driving factor. Should you tell the losing bidders the difference between their bid and the winning bid? Yes. Tell them from a percentage standpoint how much they were over on the job. Should you give them the opportunity to meet or better the winning bid? No. Generally, it's recommended that you don't. Why? Because word is likely to get out that you went beyond the regular bidding process to obtain a lower price and in the future, other printers will adjust their prices up in anticipation of this. Simply thank printers for their bids and tell them you'll be sure to include them in the bidding process for your next project.

Once you've received a formal bid, make sure that each and every aspect of the job (from beginning to end) is included (e.g., charges for such things as packaging and freight).

You should have the printer you choose put the accepted bid in writing, and you should then follow up with a purchase order that indicates the agreed-upon charges for the project. Request that any adjustments to the original bid be submitted in writing. This will make your life a lot easier when you receive the final bill and will help avoid unnecessary disputes.

There are a number of ways you can save money getting your material printed. Again, perhaps the best way is to develop a good working relationship with the printers in your area. In addition:

- Select the right printer and the right printing process. Some jobs are best suited for certain presses and can be done more economically if they're done on the right equipment.

- Consider the use of colored paper to give a two-color effect when you're using just one color of ink.

- Look into the use of stock printed material. Many suppliers offer a variety of preprinted, colorful bulletins that are very economical for short runs.

- When choosing ink color, select those colors that are offered by your printer as "standards" — mixing inks for special colors will add substantial cost to your print job.

- Avoid bleeds (areas where printing runs off the edge of the paper). These are more difficult for the printer to print and, consequently, add to the cost of your job.

- Proofread and double check everything before you send your artwork to the printer.

- Determine your mail date and then work backwards from that date to schedule due dates for creative, copy, art, type, printing, folding, labeling, and insertion.

- Build extra time into your schedule for the unexpected — always ask to receive your job at least a week earlier than you actually need it.

- Make sure your instructions (and those of your graphic designer) are clear. This will avoid errors and the need to make revisions after the proof stage; giving the printer a complete dummy, or mock-up, of your job can also be very helpful.

- When speaking to printers and getting quotes, make sure to ask how much time they need to do the job — get time commitments in writing.

- Don't forget about author alterations (AAs), changes that you make after the proofing process which you will be charged for. A good rule of thumb is to add 10 to 20 percent to the bid you receive to cover these changes.

- To help avoid delays and keep costs down, use standard paper and envelope sizes.

- Check with printers to see if they have leftover stock from prior jobs. If they do, and it will work for your job, cost savings can be substantial.

- Various parts of your job may best be handled by different printers; shop around to make sure that you're getting the best quality as well as the best price.

- If you're unhappy with the job (if it hasn't met your specs, if your proof changes weren't made, if the print quality is poor, or if the job was delivered late), talk to the printer and ask for a reprint or an adjustment to your bill — the standard compensation rate is between 10 to 15 percent of the total bill.

- Make sure that you see proofs of all jobs. With a one- or two-color job, a blueline proof is sufficient. If the job is more complicated, ask to see a color key proof. While this won't show you a true representation of the color, it will show the color breaks. It's the printer's responsibility to match your proofs, so it should not be necessary to ask for a press proof in addition to the bluelines. This will only delay the job and may add additional cost.

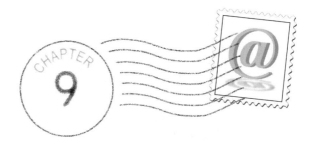

Postal Procedures and Regulations

"**M**ail" is the operative word in the term "direct mail marketing." Without a good understanding of how to mail, a direct mailer has virtually no chance of succeeding. Today, of course, mail doesn't mean just the traditional snail mail. However, that form of mail is still prevalent and still requires a basic understanding of postal rules and regulations. Fortunately, the USPS can be a great resource for information on how to be efficient and effective.

There are few private businesses and government agencies who have done more to evolve their services to meet the needs of their customers, over a longer period of time, than the United States Postal Service and Canada Post. Moving written correspondence and printed materials efficiently at the lowest possible cost has been the USPS's job since the USA was just a collection of colonies bordering the Atlantic Ocean.

In the United States, setting up the USPS was one of the first things the founding fathers did. During early colonial times, Native Americans were sometimes used to carry messages between the colonies. Benjamin Franklin was appointed the first Postmaster General in 1775; the first US Constitution wasn't written until 1776 in the midst of the American Revolution. That's how important the visionary founding fathers knew that delivery of mail and messages would be to the future of the new nation-in-waiting.

The evolution of the USPS is truly a remarkable story of business innovation to satisfy the need for the personal delivery of mail to every physical address, home, business suite, and PO box in the country. A continuous stream of new and changing services have put their signature on the USPS — the issuance of postage stamps, the Pony Express with its relay of fresh horses and riders, commemorative stamps, Rural Free Delivery, Parcel Post, airmail, zip codes, Express Mail, self-adhesive stamps, the Forever stamp, and many other fresh service introductions characterize the USPS's ongoing efforts to satisfy the needs of the American business community.

In spite of burgeoning competition from private air and surface carriers, the USPS and Canada Post are excellent business partners and economical choices to move mail and small packages and to help businesses stretch their advertising dollars by delivering sales messages through the daily mail.

If asked, chances are that not many businesses will list these national postal carriers in their annual advertising budget. However, it makes a lot of sense to set aside a portion of your advertising dollars for postal service:

- Direct mail is still a very effective method of advertising for business-to-business and business-to-consumer contact. In this age of high-tech/low-touch and the advent of Internet and social marketing, direct mail can grow your customer base by delivering your message directly to your customer's door.

- Direct mail tends to increase interest in a company's website.

- On the USPS website, there is an entire step-by-step section devoted to direct mail and developing campaigns, including detailed suggestions for how to create your mailing list and how to design your mail pieces. The Canada Post website contains a direct mail section with a similar step-by-step section as well as numerous tips and detailed best practices for direct mailing. An oversized postcard is still a very cost-effective direct mail piece that can get your message read by those you wish to target.

- Many people wait for their mail delivery daily, and many others consider their day incomplete without receiving and reading their mail. The USPS has found that 98 percent of people bring in their mail every day, and 77 percent sort through it right away. Similarly, Canada Post has found that 93 percent of Canadians read their mail the same day they receive it. That's a powerful marketing avenue you are missing if you don't do any direct mail advertising.

- You may also want to consider using a mailing service if you will be doing a large bulk mailing. The postal service can often save you 30 percent or more on postage by presorting your mail and can append all of the addresses on your US mailing list with Zip+4 codes for faster processing.

1. Efficiencies through Direct Mail

Whether your business is home-based or housed in a metropolitan high-rise, you will always have the need for mailing hard-copy correspondence or products to your customers. Especially in today's economy, it's vital to know how to do that cost-effectively.

Portals offered by some delivery companies provide the ability for mailers to process mail from their desktops — whether a print service provider that is offering a portal online, or even the USPS.

Direct mailers should not expect to pay full price for postage for their mail pieces (currently $0.44 for first-class mail). The key is to make your mail as easy as possible for the USPS to process — the more you do to automate your mailings, including using online portals to speed up processing, the deeper the discounts you can receive.

Make sure to validate the address — ensure that it's deliverable. That's done through an address matching process that is usually available through whatever portal provider you're using; in some cases for an additional fee, in some cases as part of the overall fee. The USPS provides a list of certified vendors and licensees that provide this service.[1] By using this process, mailers can tell up front whether or not they have a valid mailing address, saving themselves (and the postal service) time and, ultimately, money. Another address verification process addresses movers — the National Change of Address (NCOA) database.[2]

The NCOA[Link] product makes change-of-address information available to mailers to help reduce undeliverable mail pieces before the mail enters the mail stream. Again, this represents a savings for the postal service which is passed on to mailers through discounts for mail which has been processed through NCOA[Link]. The mailers additionally benefit from greater assurance that their mailing pieces will reach their intended destinations.

---

[1] "Certified Vendors and Licensees," www.usps.com/ncsc/ziplookup/vendorslicensees.htm, accessed March 18, 2011.
[2] "NCOALink® Systems," www.usps.com/ncsc/addressservices/moveupdate/changeaddress.htm, accessed March 18, 2011.

In addition to the wealth of readily accessible (and free) information the USPS and Canada Post websites offer for mailers, there are associations and special interest groups that direct mailers can join, often locally. The American Marketing Association (www.marketingpower.com) and the Direct Marketing Association (www.newdma.org) are good resources.

2. Business Tools

Besides the convenience of going online to USPS and having your mail placed on hold or having it forwarded to an alternate address while you're away, there are a myriad of business tools that have been developed by the USPS and Canada Post over the years by listening to what small and large business owners have said would make their life easier. Here are a few worthy of mention:

- The USPS Shipping Assistant and Canada Post Direct Marketing Online desktop applications allow you to print and ship right from your desktop or laptop computer.

- Canada Post's Brand-It program allows customers to put their business logo on prepaid postage labels.

- USPS Web Tools, a handy collection designed for the more serious shipper:

  - Address Information APIs to make sure that your mailing addresses are correct.

  - Delivery Information APIs to check estimated delivery times before mailing or to track a package after mailing.

  - Rate Calculator APIs to find out postage rates based on weight, class of mail, and origin and destination details.

  - Shipping Labels APIs to print shipping labels with free or low-fee confirmation services.

  - Carrier Pickup APIs to allow you to schedule a pickup of your packages when your mail carrier delivers your daily mail.

- Canada Post's AdCard service is designed to handle virtually all of the logistics of a customer's direct mailing campaign all the way from targeting customers to delivering the mail. The trademarked GeoPost Plus service is a free specialized tool designed to help direct mailers pinpoint the right customers and improve marketing results by tailoring messages based on customer characteristics.

- Intelligent Mail is a trademark of the USPS, and these products and services use machine-readable codes (i.e., bar codes) to identify unique pieces of mail. This gives large mailers the ability to follow the progress of their mail through the various steps of processing on the way to delivery.

- Postage payment options for businesses. Any successful business has to make it easy for customers to pay for services or products. The USPS and Canada Post do that by offering a wide range of payment options including regular, special issue, and Forever/Permanent postage stamps; prepaid Priority Mail envelopes and flat-rate boxes; postage meters that can print postage onto your mailing pieces right at your home or office; permit imprints for high-volume mailers that allow postage to be automatically deducted from their Postal Service accounts; and credit, debit, or FedWire payments.

3. What's on the Horizon for USPS and Canada Post?

It goes without saying that the USPS and Canada Post are constantly reworking methods of doing business to survive in these tough economic times. Until the Postal Reorganization Act of 1970 was adopted, the USPS was a regular, tax-supported federal government agency. Now it is mandated to be "revenue neutral," meaning it is supposed to break even and not make a profit. It also survives on the sale of postal products and value-added services since regular mail delivery is free of charge (to recipients). There have been recent public hearings on the possibility of dropping Saturday delivery as a free service to reduce costs. Canada has been receiving increasing calls for privatization or partial privatization of Canada Post along the lines of countries such as the United Kingdom, Sweden, and the Netherlands, although such efforts have met with limited success.

Beginning January 2, 2011, the USPS is loosening up the rules on simplified addressing, an effort that is expected to help small businesses who don't use the postal service for bulk mailings because it is too expensive for them. Simplified addressing allows businesses to use delivery route information instead of specific names and addresses to reach target customers in specific geographic locations.

It can lower business costs by reducing the time it takes to prepare pieces for mailing and by eliminating the need to buy mailing lists. In most instances, the simplified addressing option will let businesses address mail to "Postal Customer" when they want to completely cover a postal route with a direct mail piece. In short, a small business will now be able to target a geographic area with a mailing that was probably cost prohibitive in the past.

In Canada, AddressDoctor has recently taken steps to upgrade Canada Post's address delivery and address quality, which will help ensure Canadian addresses are accurate from the beginning of the mailing process. The new system alerts mailers immediately if they have used an address that is missing components or is otherwise flawed so that they can fix the error before putting their items in the mail, rather than having to wait for them to be returned, costing both time and money.

How to Test and Evaluate Results

Y ou've planned a campaign, ordered lists, prepared a mailing piece or online email promotional copy, distributed your campaign materials, and now you're ready to sit back, relax, and wait for responses to start rolling in.

Before you relax, though, schedule a postmortem. These casual meetings allow everybody who was involved in the project to offer their input on how the process went and what could be improved the next time. What went well? What didn't go well? What would you do differently next time? Don't wait too long to hold this meeting. You want the input while the project is still fresh in everyone's mind.

Then when responses or orders are in, you can begin to look at how successful your direct mail effort was. You need to determine if you are making money and, if you are making money, you need to know why. Is it the list? Is it the offer? Is it your copy approach? Your format? How can you tell? Through response analysis and testing. This chapter will take a close look at analyzing the response to your direct mail efforts.

1. What Is a Good Response Rate?

Don't let anyone fool you — there is no such thing as an "average" return or an average "good" return. The question most frequently asked by direct mailers, neophyte and pro alike, at direct-marketing conferences every year and in blogs all over the Internet is: "What is a good response rate?" The answer is that it depends on what you're selling, who you're selling it to, and what price you're asking for your product or service. It depends on the time of year, the economy, and the whims of your prospects. Let's look at a few examples to illustrate this point.

Joe Mailer sells a $350 product. He does a mailing to 10,000 people and receives 50 responses or a 0.5 percent return. That's terrible, you say, the response should have been at least 1 percent! But wait a minute. Let's take a look at what's really happening here:

- Revenue = 50 responses at $350 each or $17,500
- Expenses = List $65/m (per thousand) or $650
- Package = $450/m or $4,500
- Total expenses = $5,150
- Gross revenue = $12,350

Clearly, Joe Mailer has more than covered the costs of his direct mail efforts.

So, you figure, you can make money with a 0.5 percent response. The answer is, "Maybe you can and maybe you can't." Let's take a look at another example.

Sue Mailer sells a $15 product. She does a mailing to 10,000 people and receives 300 responses or a 3 percent return. "That's a terrific response!" you exclaim. But let's take a look at what this really means for Sue:

- Revenue = 300 responses at $15 each or $4,500
- Expenses = List $45/m or $450
- Package = $350/m or $3,500
- Total expenses = $3,950
- Gross revenue = $550

Knowing she has an inexpensive product, Sue was more conservative with her marketing expenses. Still, she only sees $550 in gross revenue. For Sue, this was a losing proposition, even with a 3 percent return. This doesn't even take into account backend, the response once returns and bad debt have been taken into consideration.

As you can see, percent of response is not a determining factor in the effectiveness of a mailing. While it certainly plays a role, what counts are the cost of your product and the cost of your mailing.

How can you calculate the success of your direct mail marketing efforts? By determining your break-even point and measuring success as revenue in excess of that break-even point.

2. Measuring Response

Once responses start being generated you need to begin measuring the actual effectiveness of your marketing efforts. You need to determine both where the responses or orders are coming from (so you can tell which lists and offers or formats to use again) and how profitable the mailing was. As we've already discussed, unlike other forms of advertising, direct mail allows you to easily tell where your responses are coming from and thus you're able to determine which efforts were worthwhile and which were not.

Suppose you want to know which list of the three you used for a particular direct mail effort provided the best response, or you simply want to know if a mailing was effective. To get this information, you must track the responses as they come in. The techniques you use will be different for traditional and online efforts.

2.1 Measuring traditional direct mail response

For traditional direct mail efforts, you will need to come up with a means of identifying the source of each inquiry or order. You'll never know how well your direct mail efforts work if you don't make an attempt to track results. In the old days, if you were soliciting orders only through the mail, you would have coded the order form to identify different campaign elements such as different lists used or different offers or formats used. As orders came in through the mail you would enter the code on the order form and, at the end of the campaign, you would have an indication of which lists, offers, or formats worked best.

If you accepted orders via the telephone you could simply have your call center representatives ask customers for the code on their catalogs or order forms.

Today, if you're using traditional direct mail and accepting orders online, you would ask the person ordering to indicate the code on his or her order form or mailer as part of the online ordering process.

In each of these cases you have a tangible way of determining the source of each order you receive. To get this information you could follow these steps:

- Code each aspect of the mailing you wish to measure with a unique code.

- Capture the code as orders come in — either via mail, phone, or Internet order.

- Keep track of both the number of responses and the dollar volume of responses received for each code on both a daily and cumulative basis.

- After all responses have been received and you've determined that the promotion has run its course, calculate a total response and a total revenue generated amount for each element of the promotion you wish to measure.

In direct mail, it's easy to code responses. Simply place the code on the order form when mailing a letter or brochure in an envelope or on the label itself if you've designed your mailer so your label will be returned. Always make sure you've taken steps to get this coding information back. It's a simple and common mistake for mailers to remember to key code their lists but then to place the label on an outer envelope which won't be returned. If the order form in your mailings isn't coded to correspond with the labels, you've lost your tracking information.

If you've coded your mailing correctly, you just have to wait for the order to come in to capture the information. Don't forget to make sure your phone operators ask for the code when a customer calls in an order — and that your online mailing form has a spot for this information as well. To simplify this process internally and to avoid confusion, always place the code in the same spot on your order form, catalog, or mailer.

You can use any kind of coding system you choose, but keep it short and simple. A three-character, alphanumeric system will provide you with virtually limitless codes. In addition to placing the codes on your mailing, be sure to keep a list of the codes you've used and what they were used for, so you can evaluate responses accurately. You can keep the information you get from your responses in a spreadsheet or database system which allows you to analyze the data in a number of different ways, or you can simply keep track manually. Additional columns can be added to track costs as well as revenue so that you can calculate a margin for each mailing done.

2.2 Tracking online response

Tracking online responses is even easier than tracking responses with traditional direct mail efforts. Built-in analytics contained in programs like Constant Contact (which can be used to generate email marketing campaigns) will provide you with information on how many people opened your email, how many clicked through the various links included in your email, and how many opted out of receiving future email from you (and these programs will automatically remove them from the list so you don't run afoul of CAN-SPAM regulations). You'll know when they opened it, and for B2B mailers, you can see the domain names of those who opened your email so you can tell which companies responded to your efforts. In addition, because you have this information, you can "bump it up against" your ordering information and if an order has not been received from that company, you have a ready-made list of email addresses for follow-up, representing a group that was at least intrigued enough by your offer to open your email!

Or, if your offer is based on drawing those who received your mailing to your website, consider developing a unique landing page that will allow you to easily determine the level of interest that your mailing generated.

The great value of direct mail marketing is the ability to track and quantify results. Don't miss any opportunity to capture relevant data that can help you determine how effective your direct mail marketing efforts are.

Free web analytic tools, such as Google Analytics, are readily available to help direct mailers determine how well various elements of their campaign are working. These tools can provide information on where visitors are coming from (i.e., direct to the site address, through various search engines, through links on email marketing efforts, e-letters, and postings on social media sites), how long they visit, what areas of the site they find most interesting, and which portions of the site may not be doing their job. This information can be used to make improvements that can mean the difference between a high bounce rate (which is bad) and a high lead generation rate (which is good).

Being able to see which parts of your online campaigns are generating the most interest and results will help you determine where to focus your energy or which aspects of your direct mail efforts need to be retooled.

The days of simply counting hits are long gone. Today's analytics are far more sophisticated and can be used in far better ways to assess and improve online marketing results. Sheer numbers and traffic don't mean anything unless you can convert those numbers to sales or business.

Google Analytics is easy to configure and is being continually improved to provide increasing value to users. Because full-featured web analytics packages can be very expensive, starting with a free solution such as Google Analytics can be a great way to learn which types of reporting tools are available before paying for features that may never be used.

Site analytics are only as valuable as the abilities of the person using the tool, of course. The three most fundamental metrics are: how many people you're reaching, where and how they are finding you, and what they're doing once you have their attention. The answers to these questions are easy to find:

- Measuring how many people visit a site is as easy as examining the *unique visitor* numbers. Because the same person may visit your site multiple times, comparing this number to total visits gives a measure of your visitor return rate.

- Determining where visitors are coming from can be seen by reviewing Referrer Reports. These reports will show you how much traffic you're receiving from search engines, other websites, and direct navigation. Direct navigation often results from visitors who have seen a website on a business card, brochure, or other printed material, or can indicate that a person has "bookmarked" your site.

- Exploring the question of "how" visitors come to a site involves looking at what key words and search phrases were used to find the website.

- Examining visitors' on-site behavior is also important. Bounce rate, number of pages viewed, average time spent on the site, and entry and exit page reports (an indication of where the visitors first entered the site and where they were last before they left the site) are all standard measurements in most analytics packages.

Social Media Marketing

You would have to be living in a cave to have missed out on all the buzz around social media. If you don't have a Twitter account, a Facebook fan page, or a LinkedIn profile these days, you're just not "with it." For direct marketers, social media can be an important part of the marketing mix, providing another opportunity to connect directly with people who can be narrowly targeted. One important caveat: Engaging in social media is more like a cocktail party conversation than a sales pitch. Those who attempt to sell too blatantly online will find themselves ostracized and, in some cases, kicked out of various online forums.

The traditional sales process is designed to proceed from the generation of awareness to an eventual sale and, hopefully, ongoing advocacy and positive word of mouth for the product or service. Social media can play a very important role at the beginning of these sales processes in terms of generating awareness for a product or service — particularly for small businesses or entrepreneurs with little-known products and not a lot of marketing dollars to invest. In addition, social media can help make consumers more knowledgeable about your product or service and influence perception and preference.

Your website will serve as the foundation for your social media marketing efforts, with all your online direct mail efforts through social media ultimately designed to send interested folks to your website or landing page.

Traditionally, marketers have relied on mass media (i.e., television, radio, and print advertising) during these initial stages of generating awareness, establishing perceptions, and creating preference for a product or service — whether an entirely new product or service, or a product or service that is appealing to a new audience (e.g., Coke continues to do awareness advertising to appeal to emerging markets).

1. What Social Media Can Do for You

Social media offers many companies the opportunity to establish awareness, knowledge, perception, and preference with the masses and, importantly, at significantly less cost and expense than traditional media. Social media will not be the *only* tool you use in your direct mail activities — we've already talked about how you might combine traditional direct mail with online email marketing efforts. Another component of these efforts can be social media communication activities.

While the "Big 3" of social media in the early twenty-first century are Facebook, Twitter, and LinkedIn, there are a number of niche players as well. Depending on your target audience, some of these may represent great opportunities for you. For instance, GoFISHn is a social media site for anglers, where they share fishing stories, tips, guides, and photos. If your company sells angling-related services or products, this would be a great social media site to frequent! Just as when you are selecting direct mail distribution lists, you will want to explore the various opportunities available to you to target your audience through social media networks that are focused and can connect you with interested consumers.

Keep in mind, though, that while social media may be the greatest new thing and very inexpensive, it may not be the best option for you. What is? It depends. As we've already discussed, the communication choices you make will depend on the following:

- Your goals — you want to be very specific here. What are you hoping to achieve?

- Your target market. Who is making the purchase decision? Who do you need to influence?

- Where the two intersect: Based on your goals and who you're hoping to influence, what communication options should you select?

Some of the potential goals that social media can help you achieve include:

- Raising awareness for your company and its products and services

- Establishing relationships

- Building a community

- Providing a conduit for conversation and interaction

- Improving customer service

- Generating prospects

- Generating sales

From a direct mail perspective you are likely to be most interested in raising awareness and generating prospects and sales. In order to do that effectively you must also be concerned with establishing relationships and building a community. That community represents your target audience in very much the same way as your own proprietary customer list represents a great resource for your traditional direct mail or email marketing efforts.

In fact, one key use of social media as part of your direct mail efforts is to help you generate, grow, and maintain a list of prospects that you can use in your traditional and online direct mail efforts.

2. Finding Your Focus

Just as when targeting your direct mail list efforts, as you choose which social media venues to engage in you need to consider your own unique goals and objectives. There are a variety of audiences you may wish to connect with and, again, no right or wrong answers. It's up to you. Knowing who you want to reach, and why, can help you determine which, if any, of the social media options make sense for you. One important point: You may have multiple audiences and, if you do, you may need to establish more than one account for these different audiences so that the information you're sharing is relevant to them specifically.

Social media has opened up some excellent opportunities to reach specific audiences efficiently and certainly needs to be considered as part of your promotion mix. However, you don't pick a tactic because it's a "cool" or "new" tactic, or because everybody else is using it. You pick a tactic — actually a combination of tactics — based on your goals and target audience and with consideration of your limited resources (time and money). You're going to develop a communication plan that uses a variety of tools to do the optimum job of reaching and influencing the people you need to reach and influence to achieve your objectives.

There are four primary ways in which consumers are influenced. In order of impact, they are:

1. Direct experience: customers' own interactions with your company and its products and services.

2. Word-of-mouth: the good things people hear from friends and family.

3. Media: what customers read and hear others say about your company.

4. Your advertising efforts (including direct mail).

Social media can be a great way to capitalize on and support your overall promotional efforts because it can touch upon all of these influence points. However, it's really points two and three that make social media the most powerful. Social media tools can give you a direct connection with consumers and the ability to leverage your communications with them to generate positive awareness and preference for your products and services. It can also be a good customer relationship management or customer service tool.

3. The Top Social Media Outlets

The top social media outlets in 2010 were Facebook, Twitter, and LinkedIn (not counting YouTube which is a slightly different form of social media). Each of these Big 3 offer unique options and opportunities that appeal to different types of businesses and business needs.

Again, the key is to use all of these social media tools to, ultimately, drive users to your web page or landing page to complete a prospecting or ordering process. Direct mail in the digital age!

3.1 Facebook

Facebook is a social-oriented social media site (you'll see in section **3.2** that LinkedIn is a more professionally oriented site). However, while Facebook originated among the college audience, the demographics of the site have changed significantly over the past few years, with women in the 50-plus audience representing the largest group of users, according to the Pew Research Center[1], which indicates that while social media use has grown dramatically among all age groups, older users have been the biggest group of new adopters. Use among Internet users age 50 plus nearly doubled (from 25 percent to 47 percent) from April 2009 to May 2010. By comparison, use by users ages 18 to 29 grew only 26 percent over this same time frame. Even 13 percent of adults age 65 and older indicate that they log on to social networking sites on a typical day (up from just 4 percent in 2009).

Facebook allows the opportunity for businesses to create sites that serve as quasi-home pages where they can share messages, post information and images, and interact with those who choose to "friend," "like," or "favorite" their pages.

Land's End, for instance, a very successful direct mailer, has a Facebook page for Land's End Canvas[2] with more than 78,000 people who "like" it in early 2011. These 78,000 people represent an audience that has indicated they're interested in hearing about what Land's End is doing and, by default, learning about product offerings, sales, and more. Some representative postings from Land's End on the site include:

- Need a Reason to Look Forward to Monday? How about this: This week's Editor's Pick is the Lands' End Canvas Men's Down Jacket and we're giving our fans a chance to win one! Enter here: http://bit.ly/CanvasEnter for a chance to win a Men's Down Jacket or a Women's Hooded Down Jacket. Which jacket do you like best? (Note the link takes those who click it to a landing page where they can enter the contest — *that's* direct mail in the social media environment.)

- The holidays are here, and we're just getting warmed up. Click below to check out our new Winter Style Shop, featuring a few of our favorites for the season. Enjoy secure shopping right on Facebook + Free Shipping. Brighten up, kick back, layer on, and think warm.

Land's End isn't the only retailer with a prominent presence on Facebook. Others include Gap (over 1,392,000 likes), Abercrombie & Fitch (over 4,058,000 likes), and Urban Outfitters (over 635,000 likes).

---

[1] "Older Adults and Social Media," www.pewinternet.org/Reports/2010/Older-Adults-and-Social-Media.aspx, accessed March 21, 2011.

[2] Land's End Canvas Facebook page, www.facebook.com/LandsEndCanvas, accessed March 21, 2011.

Much can be learned from the activities of these companies — as well as from companies among your competitors who have established a presence on Facebook. Monitor their sites to see what they do, the types of messages they post, and — most importantly — the responses they receive from their followers.

Note that these are all companies that can connect with people in a visual way by showing their products prominently on Facebook and offering the opportunity to click through to the website to place an order.

There is no cost for joining or participating on Facebook. Facebook does, however, offer advertising at very minimal rates which allows marketers to very specifically target those on Facebook with ads that appear on the right-hand side of the page.

3.2 LinkedIn

LinkedIn, as previously mentioned, is a more professionally oriented social media site. Originally used as a tool by both job seekers and those with jobs to fill, LinkedIn appeals to professionals in a variety of industries and is probably most noted for its large numbers of groups that provide a place for like-minded people, with interests ranging from quilting to astrophysics, to gather and share information and insights.

In 2010, LinkedIn had more than 85 million members in more than 200 countries. Its site claims that "a new member joins LinkedIn approximately every second, and about half of our members are outside the US." Executives from all Fortune 500 companies are members of LinkedIn.

When joining LinkedIn, members create a profile that summarizes their professional expertise and accomplishments. They then invite contacts to "connect" with them and their network subsequently expands exponentially because it includes their connections, as well as their connections' connections. Users can —

- create and collaborate on projects, gather data, share files, and solve problems;
- be found for business opportunities and find potential partners;
- gain new insights from discussions with like-minded professionals in private group settings;

- discover inside connections that can help them land jobs and close deals; and

- post and distribute job listings to find the best talent for their company

It's free to join and use and the basic functionality provided with the free membership is adequate for many users. Premium options are also available.

3.3 Twitter

Twitter offers visitors short bursts of information (often with links to more detail) in 140 characters or less. It's an online phenomenon that many still fail to understand (or appreciate), but that some have found useful for building loyal groups of followers and raising awareness and preference for their brands and products. Pew's research suggests that one in ten Internet users age 50 and older say they use Twitter or another service to share updates about themselves or to see updates about others.

Twitter describes itself as "an information network" and says it "connects you to the latest information about what you find interesting. Simply find the public streams you find most compelling and follow the conversations." Streams represent the list of 140-character posts that Twitter participants write. While this doesn't seem like a lot of space, Twitter notes that: "You can share a lot with a little space. Connected to each Tweet is a rich details pane that provides additional information, deeper context, and embedded media. You can tell your story within your Tweet, or you can think of a Tweet as the headline, and use the details pane to tell the rest with photos, videos, and other media content."

4. Prioritizing Your Time and Efforts

While social media can represent a lot of opportunities for some companies, it can also represent a huge investment of time and that's where the "cost" comes in. While many consider social media to be free, the truth is that "time is money." For many, the jury is still out in terms of whether that time investment is actually worth it. It *can* be, of course, but like any other communication tool, only if it's used strategically. What does that mean? That means initially establishing some specific goals and objectives and then developing strategies and tactics designed to help you achieve those objectives.

At first, your goal may simply be to understand how it works and that's a valid goal. Practicing and playing around with social media can be a good way to understand how it works and the value that it might hold for you and your business. But as you practice, practice with a purpose — and a certain amount of caution. What happens on social media, stays on social media (and the Internet), forever. Everything you say, everything you post, and everyone you follow becomes a reflection of your brand. Following are a number of practical tips that can help you maximize your social media efforts and ensure that the time you're spending online is spent in meaningful *and* measurable ways.

4.1 Pick the tools that are right for you and your audience

As we've seen, Facebook is a very socially oriented site with much focus on the use of photos.

Twitter is a micro-messaging site that lends itself primarily to one-way communication — you tweet, your followers read, and, if you're lucky, they retweet your messages. LinkedIn is a business-oriented site that can be useful for job seekers and B2B marketers.

Remember, these are just the top three. There are also a myriad of other, more specialized social media sites that can help you connect with very specific audiences.

4.2 Consider maintaining multiple sites

Many people maintain both professional and personal social media profiles that target different audiences. You may also wish to have a variety of professional or personal sites, each designed to reach a different audience and focus on different key messages. For instance, you might have a separate profile for each of a number of different product lines, or a profile for customers and a profile for prospects.

Your decisions should be based both on your objectives and the time you have available to maintain multiple profiles.

4.3 Connect with those you can learn from

Follow and friend those that you're interested in connecting with or learning from. This may include thought leaders in your industry, potential clients, or customers — or even competitors. Keep in mind that your competitors may also be following you!

Just as when establishing profiles, consider which profile should be following which people. You probably don't want to use your personal Facebook profile, for instance, to follow a key client.

4.4 Maintain a clear focus

Know what you want to get out of your social media activities and maintain a clear focus. Don't attempt with any one profile to be all things to all people. Having specific objectives will help you maximize your limited resources (primarily time). Having a specific focus will help to ensure that you're providing value to the people who choose to "friend" or "follow" you. Each profile should clearly reflect a specific brand or identity targeted to a specific audience. As you develop and deliver content, you can keep a sharp focus on what that audience expects from you and keep them connected by providing specific, relevant information.

4.5 Incorporate your social media with your website

Incorporate your social media efforts into your website, if appropriate. Once you establish a presence on some of these social media sites, you can include little icons on your website to let people know where they can find you and make it easy for them to connect with you immediately.

4.6 Keep your branding consistent

If you have a website for your online gift shop and also maintain a Twitter account and post videos to YouTube, make sure that all these channels are designed with the same "look and feel" to enhance brand identity and consistency.

4.7 Use analytics to track effectiveness

There are a variety of things you could track and measure on social media (e.g., number of followers, number of retweets, and number of clicks through to links you've posted).

The Internet offers so many great opportunities to track activity; you should be taking advantage of this data to help you determine whether or not your activities are worthwhile. What matters? It depends, of course, on your objectives. However, be careful to measure what really matters. Ultimately, it may not be the number of followers or the number of retweets you receive that represent results for you. It may be the downstream impacts of actual referrals, orders, or advertisers you attract through these activities.

4.8 Cross-pollinate

Suppose you have a website, a blog, and an e-letter that you produce on a regular basis — and you're active on Twitter and LinkedIn. These activities should not be independent. They should be carefully planned and coordinated so that you can leverage the value of your efforts. For instance, in a blog you might reference a topic that recently appeared in your e-letter, or refer to a tweet you sent recently. You might reference a relevant blog posting through Twitter and LinkedIn. When you release an e-letter update you might notify your connections through Twitter and LinkedIn. Hopefully you can see how this works. Now, this could take a lot of time and thought, but not if you develop a specific plan that outlines when and what content you will be producing through all these venues. Then it's a simple matter of following your plan.

4.9 Repurpose content to maximize the use of your time

It is unlikely that all of your connections will be reading all of your content in all the places it appears. That would be wonderful, but it's just not going to happen. So don't worry about repurposing your content across multiple platforms — a blog post can become an article in your e-letter and the basis of a tweet and a LinkedIn update. Your e-letter can include links to your blog postings, your website, articles you've written, or places you've been quoted. Your LinkedIn updates can include a link to a recent blog post, etc.

Again, make these activities part of the plan you develop to ensure that your messages are coordinated across all these channels and aligned with your overall objectives.

4.10 Get involved

LinkedIn has a feature called "groups" that allows users to connect with affinity-based listings of people across a broad range of interests and activities. Simply search for the topic or issue you're interested in and you'll find a list of groups in reverse order based on the number of participants. Request to join, and the group moderator will likely approve your request. You may also wish to set up your own groups to initiate conversations and build networks among like-minded individuals.

4.11 Streamline your social media activities

Use tools like TweetDeck and HootSuite to help streamline your social media activities. These tools allow you to post to multiple sites and profiles, schedule updates and tweets, and track the effectiveness of your online activities.

4.12 Social media may not be right for your business

Don't be embarrassed or feel uncool if you decide that social media is not for you. It may not be. Just as television advertising is not the appropriate tool for every marketer, social media may not be right for all businesses. The key to determining whether it is or not is consideration of your audience and your objectives. In any communication endeavor, those are always the only two things that matter!

The Future of Direct Mail Marketing

Nobody has a crystal ball for what the future might hold in terms of direct mail marketing and how it will continue to evolve. What is certain is that direct mailers will have a wide range of options available to them for combining the power of both traditional and online options. Creativity is the name of the game — as it always has been. As we've seen, the basics still apply: A clear idea of the target audience and the ability to reach them with a clear and compelling message.

The ability to combine traditional direct mail with websites and landing pages, email marketing, and mobile marketing means virtually limitless possibilities for companies willing to be creative. Zpizza is an example of that; in 2009, zpizza used a combination of direct mail, email, and mobile to encourage consumers to join its ztribe loyalty club. Based in California, zpizza is a gourmet pizzeria that specializes in the use of unique toppings such as shiitake mushrooms, arugula, and pears. The goal with the campaign was to identify people who would become loyalty customers and capture their information in a database that could be used to alert them to special offers and new items.

The campaign incorporated two direct mail efforts sent to consumers living within three miles of each of the chain's 86 locations — 2,800 mailers were mailed in August and 3,000 in October. The mailers included a pizza-shaped scratch-off area which revealed a code that recipients could text to the company, along with their email address, to claim a prize — no purchase required. Once recipients sent their text message they immediately received a return message alerting them to check their email to see what they'd won. That email message also included an offer to join the ztribe club.

The effort was considered a success — the August mailer generated more than 500 text-in entries and a redemption rate of 1.5 percent. In October, more than 1,400 texts were received with a similar redemption rate. Registration for the ztribe loyalty club increased by 20 percent.

These integrated efforts can be used on a much larger scale as well. Thaddeus B. Kubis, with NAK Integrated Marketing in New York City, tells of a campaign for a large airline targeted to frequent flyer business flyers who did *not* currently fly via its airline. The demographic profile was created based on existing clients and resulted in a final list of 55,000 contacts. Three personalized mailing postcards were sent to this group, each containing a PURL which linked the potential traveler to a five-page microsite (i.e., landing page). Part of the landing page offered downloads for maps and sites for Paris. Visitors were asked some questions regarding their final destination, and an eight-question survey was used to further qualify the lead. Kubis says that $1.3 million in incremental sales were directly linked to this effort.

1. An Evolution of Consumer Interaction

Sal Tripi has been with Publishers Clearing House for the past 18 years. Tripi has seen a lot of changes over those years in his role handling compliance, privacy, and operations, and is trusted and respected for his insight on email marketing practices.

In the "old days," Tripi handled lettershop, warehousing, the payment process, inbound order processing, inventory forecasting, and merchandising. He made the transition from offline to online about seven years ago.

"The big difference between online and offline is really being able to offer one-to-one marketing with consumers," says Tripi; information that is "targeted and tailored just for that individual."

This ability is made possible by the significant amounts of data that are generated and collected by businesses as consumers engage with various websites. This explosion of data gathering and access to information, says Tripi, has led to greater privacy concerns among consumers and greater responsibility for online marketers. "Consumers are uneasy about this so transparency and putting choice into consumers' hands is very, very important," says Tripi, who acknowledges that the privacy concerns in the online and offline worlds are very different.

"Online data is much easier to exploit because of the relatively low cost associated with executing campaigns," Tripi says. A marketer in the offline world, he notes, has a significant investment in terms of buying and brokering lists, printing, and mailing costs. "In the online world the investment is so small that unscrupulous marketers have exploited that opportunity and that's created the need for things like CAN-SPAM," he says.

It also makes the process of marketing online different in terms of how lists are attained and used. "In the online world you're really asking a third party to present your offer in front of a user," he says. "In the traditional direct mail world you acquire the name and you send them the mailing."

While it's not illegal to just buy an email distribution list and mail it, says Tripi, "it is a very, very bad practice and one that we would never, ever engage in." Online marketers are much better off using a trusted third party to deliver the offer, and those who are concerned about their brand, their image, their relationships with consumers, and their customers do just that.

Deliverability is also noticeably different online than via the traditional route, with a gatekeeping function that really doesn't exist in the offline world outside the business environment. "Imagine the local post office having the ability to throw out mail that they think the consumer doesn't want to receive," says Tripi. "That's really the online world of email. The individual ISPs make decisions that they think represent the best interests of their consumers." So, much of the mail that marketers are attempting to send to a recipient may be intercepted along the way and never reach the target at all (similarly to how a mail room or administrative assistant might intercept the mail intended for business executives).

Why is this okay in the online world? Because, says Tripi, the ISPs work for the consumers, not the mailers. In the offline world, USPS works for the mailers.

Deliverability — the ability to get your mail delivered to its intended recipient — is a first-level measure of direct mail effectiveness, even though as Tripi points out, this isn't really a measure of consumer behavior.

Another important measure is whether or not consumers have engaged with the mail. That's a measure that really can't be monitored in the offline world. Mailers really have no idea whether or not the consumer looked at or interacted with the mail piece unless they get a response, which is quite different than online! When an email is received, online marketers can tell whether it was opened, what links were clicked, and how long a consumer engaged in exploring various parts of a landing page or website. "There are industry statistics out there that indicate that average click rates range anywhere from 5 percent to 15 percent in terms of consumers engaging with an email," says Tripi, who adds that Publishers Clearing House's average is 35 to 40 percent. Greater engagement is, among other things, an indication of engagement!

Tracking is obviously much easier online. In the offline world, marketers don't know what, if anything, happened with their mailing until the consumer responds in some way (e.g., calling an 800 phone number or returning an order form). Online, says Tripi, "You get to see who took the mail and threw it out immediately, who said 'I don't want to see anymore,' who was offended and reported it as spam, and who engaged with it."

Still, Tripi notes, online marketing has not yet and may never entirely replace traditional direct mail marketing. "When email first came out they said 'this will be the death knell of direct mail,'" he says. "Then social media came out and they said 'this will be the death knell of email.' And now mobile is emerging and they're saying 'okay, this is *really* going to be the death of everything before it.'" However, Tripi asserts, "All of these things are complementary communication channels that allow marketers and consumers to interact in a variety of ways. Multi-channel marketing has the ability to drive communications in the way the consumer wants to interact." Ultimately, he says, "Respecting the consumers means giving them transparency and choice into what's happening to them with their communication experiences."

2. What the Experts Have to Say

Obviously, nobody knows for sure what the future holds for direct mail marketers, but here's a round-up of what experts and participants in the field had to say in late 2010:

Ken Fitzgerald, executive creative director; and Michael Osborn, managing director of Catalyst (www.catalystinc.com)

The future of direct marketing hinges on the ability to adapt and evolve with emerging marketing channels. There will no longer be a "mail only" channel. If there is, it will fail. Why? Because the customers are in control. They dictate how, when, and in what channel they will accept your message. If your direct strategy isn't intrinsically linked to other channels, you run the risk of alienating your customer or having them miss your message altogether.

A strong direct strategy will enhance all other marketing efforts because of segmentation, personalization, and having the ability to craft more relevant copy and offers to the customer. That ability to be measurable and accountable is the hallmark of a strong direct-marketing strategy.

In the future, marketing will become a blur. The contact strategy will become intuitive to include a variety of channels that will build on each other's messaging — thereby becoming direct channels themselves. Other channels will begin to adapt direct-marketing strategies and begin to collect data that will make them smarter in their approach to messaging, content, personalization, and analytics. The concept of any type of "blast" or "mass" will disappear.

The invaluable foundation of direct marketing is analytics. The ability to collect information on a targeted group and mine for individual data allows for prosciutto-thin segmentation. That enables the creative to be more relevant and more effective.

Strong analytics opens a world of possibilities that goes beyond creative. Offer strategies that will resonate stronger. Contact strategies can also be effective because if your message is spot-on you might not have to contact the customer as often. A strategic database is worth its weight in gold. Now your copy is a conversation not a lecture or brochure-ware. The visuals reflect their lifestyle and sensibilities. The brand is not talking to them, and not at them. They will feel that this message was created "for me." The days of "low interest" or "high interest" categories are over. We are now in the age of "My Interest."

In the future, we have to listen harder, not shout louder.

Carolyn Goodman, president and creative director of Goodman Marketing Partners (www.goodmanmarketing.com)

As long as there's the ability to build accurate and highly targeted lists, and an efficient method to reliably deliver mail to a target's mailbox or email inbox, direct mail and email will live a long and healthy life. Buyers consume content from multiple sources and channels as a way to build their knowledge, increase awareness of, and form impressions of a brand or solution to their problems. Direct mail and email continue to support and enhance marketing communication efforts in ways that yield a better combined return on investment (ROI) than any single media channel. Not everyone consumes content the same way or wants to receive content through the same channel. Those who divert their marketing efforts to focus on the latest, hottest media while ignoring direct mail and email will discover their results less than optimized.

Shel Horowitz, author, speaker, and consultant (http://shelhorowitz.com)

As email continues to decline in effectiveness, *smart* companies will return to postal direct mail, but take advantage of digital-style segmentation and technology. Rather than waste 50 cents or a dollar per envelope mailing to non-prospects, I expect that more companies will use small, extremely niched lists that will produce high returns if opened (always a challenge) and very high lifetime customer value.

I also think more companies will begin to use a strategy I've advocated for years — mail not to prospects but to influencers. For example, a publisher could mail to bookstore owners and librarians who will influence the purchase of many books.

To get those letters opened? How about preceding it with either a phone call or postcard? With phone, you'd only mail to those who wanted your offer, and your envelope would say: "Thank you for asking to see this in our phone call of (date)."

Alex Malagon, Partner in Credelis Media Group, Inc. (CMG) (www.credelis.net)

In this fast-paced digital age, industries must stay adaptable to trends and technology as new opportunities arise. I have been a leader in the printing industry in South Florida for 14 years. CMG provides "Outernet" solutions for a variety of market segments. Solutions range in scope from digital signage to touch-screens. In March of this year, my company became the first and only media company to become an exclusive partner with Total Immersion and offer Augmented Reality to our clients. We, along with market analysts, believe Augmented Reality is the future of direct mail.

Technology has allowed for traditional print direct mail to reach the digital arena through Augmented Reality. Companies can now extend the reach and impact of their direct mail campaign by choosing to use Augmented Reality. What the technology does is integrate 3D objects into live video, mixing real and virtual worlds together instantly. For instance, if our client — a cell phone carrier — wants to promote a new model of mobile phone, it could use Augmented Reality to display the phone's features. The direct mail recipient would receive a traditional mail piece and be prompted to visit a website. As long as the mail recipient has a camera on their computer, the technology can take the embedded image in the printed piece and make it appear in 3D on the recipient's computer screen. This technology has endless possibilities and offers companies a chance to be interactive with their target audience, which ultimately makes the recipient's action more likely.

Dan Smith, senior vice president of marketing for ClickSquared (www.clicksquared.com), an email and cross-channel database marketing company

No, direct mail is not dead. While it may not be the mainstay of communication programs that it once was, it is still a very viable channel that marketers can use to reach customers and prospects as part of an integrated cross-channel marketing solution. In my opinion, *any* marketing tool loses its effectiveness when seen as a stand-alone solution. Many organizations make the mistake of segregating *inbound* marketing efforts (usually online marketing such as search engine marketing or search engine optimization) from *outbound* marketing (better known as database marketing, with execution including email or direct mail, for instance). The truth is, a good campaign leverages both for a variety of reasons:

- Not all customers respond to communications in the same way. Some are much more likely to respond to email while others will only reply to direct mail.

- For customers whose email addresses you don't have, direct mail is a great way to drive people to your website to collect their email addresses and enhance your existing database.

- Depending on regulations specific to your industry, there is certain information that can only be sent via direct mail.

- Direct mail won't make sense for all customers and prospects in all situations but it is an integral part of cross-channel marketing — and it's certainly not dead.

Resources

Following are a number of resources available online and offline to provide you with additional information about the ever-changing world of direct mail marketing, and more.

Magazines (and Their Associated Online Sites)

- *BtoB* — The Magazine for Marketing Strategists: www.btobonline.com

- *Direct Marketing News*: www.dmnews.com

Blogs and Websites

- Email Marketing Reports: www.email-marketing-reports.com

- *The Huffington Post*: www.huffingtonpost.com

- MarketingProfs: www.marketingprofs.com

- Practical Ecommerce — Insights for Online Merchants: www.practicalecommerce.com/articles/1976-Six-Pointers-for-Formatting-Your-Ecommerce-Emails

- Web Pro News: www.webpronews.com